PELICAN BOOK A708

Jack Ponterory
2011

10/11

2.50

PAINTING IN ENGLAND
1500–1880

DAVID PIPER

Painting in England 1500-1880

an introduction by David Piper   Penguin Books

Penguin Books Ltd, Harmondsworth, Middlesex, England
Penguin Books Inc., 3300 Clipper Mill Road, Baltimore 11, Md, U.S.A.
Penguin Books Pty Ltd, Ringwood, Victoria, Australia

Painting in England 1500–1870 first published by The Book Society 1960
Painting in England 1500–1870 first published with additional material as
Painting in England 1500–1880 in Pelican Books 1965

Copyright © David Piper, 1960, 1965

Made and printed in Great Britain by Balding & Mansell Ltd, Wisbech
Set in Monotype Times

Contents

Acknowledgement

The publishers wish to express their gratitude to all the galleries and private collectors who have kindly given permission for their paintings to be reproduced in this volume, details of which are to be found in the Sources of Illustrations at the end of the book.

The Sixteenth Century

The luxury of having non-utilitarian furniture about the house – furniture that is not for sitting on or for storing things in, but is purely ornamental – was acclimatized only relatively late in England. Painted pictures – 'wall-furniture' – are one kind of such ornament; we are so accustomed to them now, that a wall can look bare without them, but it was not always so. In the Middle Ages, painting was hardly ever conceived in order simply to give pleasure; it was functional and educative, and its subjects were normally not of the here but of the hereafter. On the walls of churches the frescoes unrolled the Bible stories, and in the breviaries, the brilliant miniatures were, so to speak, aids to gracious praying. Only at the Renaissance did the art of painting begin to specialize in more avowedly aesthetic pleasure, contracting off the church walls and the altars into easel paintings, and setting up a portable world of its own within the gold frame. Its subjects too became more mundane, and concentrated on man in his earthly setting; a revival of interest in presenting an illusion, both of man in all the pride of flesh and life and of the three-dimensional world in which he lived, precipitated the rediscovery of the necessary technique of best achieving that illusion – the artifice of perspective, known to the Greeks and the Romans, but abandoned (doubtless as irrelevant to their purposes) by the Middle Ages. The technique of painting in oil was developed, permitting a much greater brilliance and subtlety in colour and modelling. These techniques were first exploited fully in the Netherlands, by painters like the Van Eycks, and in Italy; by 1500 the three giants of the High Renaissance were already at the beginning or in the middle of their careers – Leonardo da Vinci, Raphael, and Michelangelo.

But about that time England was, in matters of material civilization as of geography, on the fringe of Europe. Except for rare moments in history she has always tended not to initiate, in matters of art, but to tag along some way behind. But it is also very difficult to formulate any valid judgement of what painting was going on in England at this time, because so much of it was subsequently deliberately destroyed by the Puritans. What is left suggests that a somewhat out-of-date imitation of Netherlandish painting was fashionable, but it is also clear that the English aristocracy had not yet acquired the habit of decorating the walls and cabinets of great private houses with paintings. Apart from religious paintings, such pictures as there were, were functional, and they were probably mainly portraits. The first English king of whom there remain any considerable number of portraits is Henry VII; he was concerned, after the Battle of Bosworth in 1485, to stamp his image on his subjects' minds as that of king in fact, thereby helping to obscure the most questionable problem as to whether he was also king by right. Such paintings had a quite specific purpose, as did the pictures of princesses that their fathers, seeking advantageous alliances, sent with details of dowries to the most promising bachelors.

The first full impact upon English eyes of the startling possibilities of Renaissance painting was that of the Swiss-German painter, Hans Holbein, between 1527 and his death in London in 1543. Holbein was one of the greatest artists of the European Renaissance; the especial characteristic of his genius was perhaps his unmatched skill in reconciling the brute facts, down to the minutest detail, of the physical appearance of the world [1] with the rigorous demands of that purely pictorial construction that supports all great works in the Renaissance tradition [2]. This skill was allied with a deep knowledge and understanding of the wealth of imagery, inspired by classical examples from Greece and Rome, that the Italian artists had created. (His virtuosity here can best be appreciated in the minutely complex and fluent decorations on his design for jewellery and goldsmiths' work, for which many drawings survive, and in his woodcuts.) But what must have shocked and delighted the relatively unsophisticated courtiers of Henry VIII, is the sheer sleight-of-hand magic of the illusion; nothing of this vividness and solidness had

1. Hans Holbein. Detail from *The Ambassadors*, 1533 (National Gallery, London)

2. Hans Holbein. *Sir Thomas More*, 1527 (29¼ by 24¾ in, 74·3 by 62·9 cm; Frick Collection, New York)

been seen in England before. It so happened that Holbein only began to be employed by Henry VIII himself when the English Reformation was well under way. Until then, the Church had been the dominant patron of the arts; now, as all image-making in religion was anathema to Protestants, artists had to seek patronage from the laity. In painting, this patronage demanded above all portraits of itself, and in England the emphasis on portraiture remained constant for the next two hundred years.

There was of course in the palaces and the grander houses a demand for decorative painting, and a newly sumptuous scale of living was set by Cardinal Wolsey in his palaces at Hampton Court and York Place (later Whitehall). At Wolsey's fall in 1530, Henry annexed these and proceeded from where Wolsey had left off. His expansion of Whitehall, and above all his building of the now completely vanished Nonesuch, were in direct emulation of Francis I's exercises in magnificence as at Fontainebleau. But the paintings for these palaces, with the exception of Holbein's great celebration of the Tudor dynasty at Whitehall (the cartoon for part of which survives in the National Portrait Gallery) were mainly decorative. Also the English climate is stubbornly hostile to wall-paintings on plaster, which is very vulnerable to damp: only fragments from the period survive. From the point of view of the painters, who have also to eat, the branch of painting offering the steadiest rewards was portraiture. Yet, while the art seemed to have been dealt a heavy blow from the one side in the loss of church patronage, from another it received encouragement; Henry VIII was a European potentate very much of his time, and conscious of European fashions of demonstrating princely magnificence. Paintings had become part of the décor of European monarchy, and Henry VIII's inventories show that he was aware of it. From his example, the fashion slowly spread, and, once rooted, it was to go on spreading ever more widely as the standard of living rose.

We are lucky to have so great an artist as Holbein as the first monument in our modern painting, yet it is curious how isolated he stands. For, in terms of artistic style and its development in painting, he had surprisingly little influence – there is no real English school developing out of his work. The reason probably lies again in the peripheral nature of English art; Englishmen, out on the fringe, tended not so much to develop on their own, as – in art as in costume – to reach in as it were, into the seething centre of the Continent, and to grab thence the latest styles – and the latest practitioners of those styles. Thus between 1500 and about 1730 the dominant styles in English painting are with one exception all imported, and so too the dominant artists tend to be foreigners.

The first painter of consequence after Holbein was a Fleming who signed his pictures H E (generally though most insecurely identified

3. Hans Eworth. *Sir John Luttrell*, 1550 (43¾ by 32½ in, 111·1 by 82·6 cm; Luttrell Collection, Dunster Castle)

as one Hans Eworth from Antwerp; the varying forms of 'his signature belong to two or perhaps more different artists). The paintings associated with him range between about 1540 and 1575. Already no longer of the High Renaissance, they show the Flemish version of the style that succeeded it – Mannerism; that is, the -ism based on the later manner of Michelangelo's style, a strained, exaggerated style that reacted against the classic balance and poise of Raphael. In the painting [3] shown here (a copy of about 1590 of a now battered original dated 1550), all the characteristics of this style are deployed and with fascinating if ultimately unconvincing ingenuity wedded to a very realistic portrait head. As an illusion, although details are fairly naturalistically painted, it does not add up; it is an allegory in picture, and the pictorial values are subordinated to the message. Much of its meaning is now lost, but we know it to represent Sir John Luttrell, soldier and trader (he died at Woolwich, of 'the sweat', in the year this was painted, when preparing for an expedition to Morocco). The goddess in the clouds appears to be Peace, extending a helping hand (her attendants have already salvaged his money bags, his warhorse and arms, from the storm) but the import is obscure, and various mottoes inscribed about the picture do not enlighten. This sort of portrait does not seem to have caught on with many clients, and later portraits associated with Eworth point in style to a uniquely English development of European Mannerism, in the work of the English-born miniaturist Nicholas Hilliard and of the Elizabethan court-painters. In them, a certain emphasis on linear design, rather than on modelling in the round, is evident; the aim seems to be, not so much to catch a sitter's physical likeness, as to demonstrate him almost like a theorem, as a cipher of rank, blood, and fashion [4]. This trend reaches a climax in the portraits of Elizabeth herself; she appears as a stiff, quasi-religious image, set up in an airless niche for adoration. Her portraits, particularly those of the last twenty-five years of her reign, are of the lineaments of majesty, not of her individual femininity; her significance is blazoned with the precise and detailed brilliance of heraldic painting. Many of the late Elizabethan and Jacobean wholelength portraits are coldly and rather frighteningly impressive, almost Byzantine in their tall remoteness, encrusted with jewels and resonant with symbols and emblems. If on a life-size scale the method

4. English School. Detail from *Queen Elizabeth I*, c. 1575
(National Portrait Gallery, London)

is sometimes also very vapid, when concentrated to miniature by
Hilliard it produced some lyrical images of an unrivalled jewel-like
purity and brilliance.

Hilliard's miniatures are mostly of the head and shoulders only,
and though always extremely stylized, trap a phantom of intimacy, of
individual and lonely life, that is almost a fragrance. Their purposes
were often indeed most intimate, for they were keepsakes, exchanged
by lovers; they were also personal jewellery housed in precious
lockets (jesting, Queen Elizabeth wore Robert Cecil, Earl of Salis-
bury, on her shoe). They alone, in Elizabethan visual art, rival the
lyric poetry of the age in their cool intricacy, their brilliant contrivance, and their melancholic passion: transiency itself drawn on

5. Nicholas Hilliard. *Unknown Youth*, c. 1590 (5⅜ by 2⅜ in,
13·7 by 6 cm; Victoria and Albert Museum, London)

14

an inch and a half of vellum, laid down on an oval often cut from a playing card. Tokens of surrender or assertions of arrogant personality?

> O God! from you that I could private be!
> Give me myself and take yourself again.

The famous miniature reproduced here [5] is more elaborate, and surely Hilliard's masterpiece; far from photographic, it is nevertheless a supremely apt realization of a lovelorn hero, perhaps from one of Shakespeare's earlier plays – this could be Benedick or Mercutio. In fact, it may well represent the Earl of Essex,* tangled in a symbolic and thorny rose-thicket of love for his virgin queen, in his golden youth before ambition went sour on him.

*The circumstantial evidence for identification as Essex, though far from conclusive, is rather stronger than that put forward recently by Leslie Hotson in support of an identification as Shakespeare's Mr W. H. (William Hatliffe?) of the Sonnets.

Van Dyck

This court-style, at once precious and remote and already archaic as a gilt fly in amber, flourished up to the reign of Charles I, but alongside it a more fleshly and naturalistic vision began to intrude – yet another immigrant style that in the end literally liquidated the old one: the Baroque. To the eye of hindsight, the Baroque in Europe appears as a thaw in the cramp of tensions that is characteristic of Mannerist art; in contrast with the latter, the work of Rubens or of Bernini seems almost as free and as violent in movement as a moving film after a series of stills. In southern Europe, the style was nurtured by, and was the instrument of, the Catholic Counter-Reformation, a luxurious, sometimes even morbid, exaltation of the Catholic faith through the senses; in the North, in its greatest achievement, the late portraits of Rembrandt, it took the form of an extraordinary interrogation, in paint as sombre and rough and as glowing as jewels on a reliquary, of the shape of human identity, a revelation of spiritual mystery in gross matter. It was, curiously, not this Northern, Protestant, and bourgeois interpretation that took root in England, but that of Catholic court-art. The swing in English taste is visible in the first years of the century, when Hilliard in his last years faded in popularity in contrast with the more naturalistic miniatures of his former pupil Isaac Oliver; in these, personality, which with Hilliard is distilled to an intellectual and spiritual essence, becomes more of a physical drama, solidly projecting from the frame in light out of shadow, a method that was specifically rejected by Hilliard. The life-scale court portraits too, in the hands of immigrant painters who imported the new style from the Low Countries, Van Somer and Mytens, take on a new weight, a lifelike presence, and a new naturalness. But distinguished and splendid though the best of Mytens' portraits are, the establishment of high

6. Sir Anthony Van Dyck. *Sir Thomas Hanmer*, c.1638 (42 by 37 in, 106·7 by 94 cm; Collection of the Earl of Bradford)

Baroque painting in England is due above all to the Fleming, Van Dyck, on his arrival here in 1631. Van Dyck was the servant of the King, Charles I, and perhaps even more of his queen, the French Catholic, Henrietta Maria. Van Dyck had worked, as a young colleague, with Rubens; he had painted in Genoa the power and dignity of the Italian aristocracy. The England to which he came was Protestant, abhorring religious images, and his output of religious painting ceased; but England, and in particular the court in which he worked, was still an absolutist monarchy fatally stubborn in its belief in the Divine Right of all kings and particularly of Stuart kings. Van Dyck's characterization of the Cavaliers has a sort of melancholy, sometimes even severe, yet lyrical voluptuousness [6]; his portraits of the King himself seem in retrospect (Van Dyck died just before the outbreak of the Civil War) to prophesy the royal martyrdom – they could almost, as a later English painter commented, serve as models for the portrait of Christ Himself. As perhaps no other painter, Van Dyck has passed into English history; it is in his vision that the romantic, brilliant, and doomed generation of the Cavaliers still lives, and his view must inevitably condition to some extent that of any historian of the period. In comparison with the inanimate display-boxes of the Elizabethan portraits, in Van Dyck's it is as though a window had been opened; a faint breeze ripples through the picture, everything is in movement. Silks and laces shimmer in light, and the picture space opens back into green landscapes, to the shifting sky, along strongly stressed diagonals; the flesh is iridescent, almost breathing. Like Holbein's, Van Dyck's genius in portraiture owed much to his power of marrying a most precise, individual characterization into a grand pictorial design, but with him the design is open and sensuous, moving with an easy and supremely elegant rhetoric. His elegance and his sensuousness enliven the paint itself; his paint seduces [7], and it has seduced countless English painters ever since – as Gainsborough said on his death-bed: 'We shall all go to heaven, and Van Dyck is of the company.'

Van Dyck was not the only symptom of what was in fact a very rich general efflorescence of the arts in England which was due, for the first time in the history of the visual arts in post-Renaissance England, to a deliberate, informed, and very intelligent patronage, primarily that of the King himself. Charles not only created a collection of Old Master paintings that was one of the finest ever brought together, but actively patronized living artists: the Italian Gentileschi painted ceilings for Inigo Jones's Queen's House at Greenwich; minor but distinguished Netherlanders like van Poelenburgh, Lievens, and the Steenwycks worked for him, and even for a brief spell Rubens himself, helping to create a décor for a court as sophisticated, brilliant, and perhaps as unreal as the masques by Ben Jonson

7. Sir Anthony Van Dyck. Detail from *Sir Thomas Hanmer*

and Inigo Jones which were its delight – a dream of splendour which burst on the harsh reality of civil war in the sixteen-forties. Van Dyck died in 1641 ; his only rival of stature, William Dobson, survived him only by five years – a strange five years of art flourishing in armed camp, for Dobson was the painter of the Cavaliers embattled, metamorphosed from butterfly courtiers into soldiers, gorgeous still, but at times with a brutal, almost meaty whiff of combat. His paint, much influenced by that of the great Venetian masters in which Charles I's collection was so rich, is broken and coarse compared with Van Dyck's, almost barbaric in texture, and even when not painting soldiers his characters stand forth as full-blown, even gross, English country gentlemen [8].

The victory of the Parliamentarian cause did not work a revolution in art as it had done in politics; it would have been surprising

8. William Dobson. *Endymion Porter*, *c.* 1642 (59 by 50 in, 150 by 127 cm; Tate Gallery, London)

if it had done so, for the two by no means necessarily go hand in hand. But the conservatism of the new men of power in art is sometimes almost startling. Their chosen painter was Robert Walker, and Walker painted them not merely *à la Van Dyck*, but often was happy simply to copy portraits by Van Dyck of fallen idols like Charles I's standard-bearer Sir Edmund Verney, or even of Charles I himself; the only difference is that a Roundhead now rides on a Cavalier body, a transposition that becomes positively macabre when the body is that of the beheaded Charles and the head Cromwell's. The fact, as Walker and his patrons recognized, is that Van Dyck had created a completely satisfactory 'glass of fashion and mould of form' for top people of the seventeenth century, images of power and distinction that were not to be bettered. Unfortunately, technically, Walker was a painter of very mediocre power. But there was at work already during the Interregnum another painter of more considerable powers, the Dutchman Peter Lely. His real triumph came during the Restoration however, and the painter to whom one turns for a sharp and vivid glimpse of reality in the fifties is not a painter of life-size portraits, but a miniaturist, Samuel Cooper.

Samuel Cooper

That Samuel Cooper is the greatest English-born painter of the seventeenth century there can be no question. He tends in general surveys to be glossed over, partly because, simply, he worked on a small scale, and partly because his art is so direct in impact that it seems to need no comment. He is not of course among the order of the greatest; you will not find in his work that intimation of the tragedy of the human condition that haunts the painting of Rembrandt, but he stands very high in the second rank of European portraitists, and he and Hilliard are the only English painters who, before Hogarth, achieved an international reputation. What starts out of almost all his miniatures is an amazing and amazed apprehension of the miracle of being alive in a given space, a given form, a given time; an acute awareness and delight in the quirk and freak of character that differentiate one human being from another [9]; most society painters paint towards the common norm of fashion rather than away from it. It was Cooper in his portrait of Cromwell, and not Lely as the legend has it, who really painted his sitter 'warts and all'. He was a painter of the most exact purity of eye; even when, after the Restoration, he came to limn the features of Charles II's mistresses, he painted them seriously and objectively and not, as did all other painters, as literal pin-up girls. His vision was matched by a technique particularly astonishing in its fusion of the minute with broadness of handling; as Horace Walpole remarked, his miniatures could be enlarged to life-scale and still not suffer from comparison with a Van Dyck. In fact, in his miniatures, he achieved a movement and freedom of design comparable with that with which Van Dyck had revolutionized the life-scale portrait. But still they are essentially miniature, a concentration, or a distillation rather, of essentials of character. In the century after his death the miniature was to suffer almost complete eclipse, for after him it became a society portrait in small, entirely conventional.

9. Samuel Cooper. *Unknown Woman*
(2⅝ by 2¼ in, 6·7 by 5·7 cm;
Fitzwilliam Museum, Cambridge)

Painting under the later Stuarts

When Charles II returned from exile (some of it spent in the most sophisticated court in Europe, that of Louis XIV) in 1660, he brought in, as Evelyn rather primly observed, 'a politer way of living which passed to luxury and intolerable expense'. The coarsening of moral tone in the court of Charles II compared with that of his father is almost as marked in the painting of the time as it is in the chronicles of the period, such as Grammont's, or in the Restoration comedies. In style the painting is broadly within the tradition, the European Baroque, of which Van Dyck was the fountainhead in England, and which dominated English painting for a century after his death (even Dobson, so different in mood, is generally within that tradition), though it perhaps never, except in Van Dyck, became fully acclimatized. To Van Dyck the Fleming succeeded Sir Peter Lely the Dutchman, the dominant painter until his death in 1680. In Lely's work, the early morning subtleties of Van Dyck are modulated into a coarser mode, sonorous in colour, opulent, fleshy in paint [10] – a perfect recording of the worldly court of Charles II. One does not look for niceties of characterization in Lely ; he is rather an extremely able decorator, his people mythological figures afloat in a warm tide of draperies and ripely buoyant flesh, his women even on occasion pornographic. To understand Restoration portraiture, you need really to see it *en masse*, as for example at Ham House ; then its rhythms, echoing from painting to painting and through the broad gold scalloping of the frames, can make an extraordinary effect. Lely at his best was more Dutch (as in his sturdy series of portraits of sea-captains, in the National Maritime Museum) than either English or French ; but much of the painting of the time was French-inspired. In England, as elsewhere in Europe, the allure and glamour of the example of the French court at Versailles was

10. Sir Peter Lely. *Comtesse de Grammont*, c. 1665 (50 by 40 in, 127 by 101·6 cm; Hampton Court Palace)

11. Sir James Thornhill. The Painted Hall, Greenwich

irresistible. Some French painters worked in England, like Gascars, but unfortunately mostly of the worst of their kind, in a purely modish display of court gallantries. The real native accomplishment in the visual arts during the reigns of the later Stuarts was of course to come in architecture – with Wren, Vanbrugh, and Hawksmoor – but there should not be forgotten, if only as phenomena, the outbreak of lavish decorative painting that these new walls afforded opportunity for. This again was largely French-inspired, and to begin with, in the persons of Verrio and Laguerre, mainly executed by direct importations from France. (Both these artists had worked under Lebrun in Paris before coming to England.) The purpose of European Baroque wall-painting on the grand scale was always illusionistic – to counterpoint the architectural enclosure of a given space, even at points to break through it, offering shafts through which a populous heaven or Arcadia became visible, a seeming extension of the mundane room, to which it lent an extra dimension. Partly because the greatest artists in this genre have never worked in England, and partly because there is something both in the relatively small human proportions of English architecture and in the English atmosphere (not only damp, which physically destroys fresco) which is alien to the illusion, nearly all wall-painting in England remains patently fictitious, and as Pope observed, Verrio's figures 'sprawl' about walls and ceilings, and refuse to take off into the upper air of the imagination. Many of them have vanished (including an illuminating suite at Windsor, where in his state apartments, Charles II displayed a curiously forthright realization in picture of the tenacious Stuart principle of Divine Right), but in great palace houses like Hampton Court, Burghley, Marlborough House, and Blenheim they can still be seen, always a little disappointing in the presence after photographs which lend them a depth and atmosphere invisible to the naked eye. The only considerable native master in this art was Sir James Thornhill, and his decoration of the Painted Hall at Greenwich [11], a truly noble room for once ample enough for the occasion, is the most rewarding and convincing specimen remaining, particularly after its recent cleaning. Thornhill had a seeming endless power of invention and a much lighter touch than Verrio or Laguerre.

In 1688 the reign of the sons of Charles I collapsed when the Catholic James II fled to exile, and a sterner spirit settled about the

12. Sir Godfrey Kneller. *Congreve*, 1709 (36 by 28 in, 91·4 by 71 cm; National Portrait Gallery, London)

English court; Dutch William III withdrew from the lavish precincts of Whitehall to the almost middle-class home built for him by Wren at Kensington, and devoted most of his energies to the destruction of Louis XIV, a process to be consummated by Marlborough under Anne. In sympathy with this more serious régime a severer note creeps into society portraiture; the draperies subside, and men and women once again become visible in their ordinary everyday dress. To the Dutchman Lely succeeded the German-born Sir Godfrey

13. William Van de Velde the Elder. *Drawing*, 1681 (6 by 16½ in,

Kneller, baronet, commanding English portrait painting for forty years between 1680 and 1720; a leaner, more astringent talent, yet generalizing the features of his sitters even more ruthlessly until one may be hard put to distinguish one sitter from another: the painter of the high, aloof mask of the Augustan age, long-nosed, plain, and plump in the shadow of the heavy foliage of the wig [12]. There were of course many lesser painters of portraits in the age of Lely and Kneller, some of them of enough distinction, like Gerard Soest, Michael Wright, John Riley, and Closterman, to give an element of individuality, of cool poetry even, to the very conventional formulas according to which they displayed their sitters; the dominant formulas are nevertheless those of Lely and Kneller. By their time, portraiture was developing almost along mass-production lines; the demand, among the aristocracy and the ever-increasing and prosperously furnished middle classes, was becoming so great that some

15 by 41·9 cm; National Maritime Museum, Greenwich)

such solution was forced upon the most fashionable painters. The master himself, while remaining in control of the overall design, painted perhaps no more than the head; the repetition by Lely and Kneller of identical poses and even of identical costumes for different sitters suggests that the sitter could choose his pose from a book of designs. Guided by drawings and no doubt personal supervision, the studio assistants would carry out most of the painting – Kneller even seems to have had specialists in drapery, flowers, and architecture. The painting of the head normally shows the individual brilliance of his own hand, a considerably greater subtlety in characterization than would sometimes be suspected from the finished object, but it also represents as much as he was personally responsible for in many of the finished products. With his successors the practice became even more mechanical, and about twelve of London's leading painters in the first half of the eighteenth century, including the most fashionable

14. Willem Van de Velde the Younger. *Drawing*, 1700 (8¾ by 12 in, 22·2 by 30·5 cm; National Maritime Museum, Greenwich)

one, Thomas Hudson, came to rely on one expert (Joseph van Aken) to paint the draperies of their portraits. Inevitably the finished product lost in vitality and freshness, and tended to become stiff, monotonous, and deadly formal.

By this time however other branches of painting were in demand besides portraiture; pictures were securely established as necessary furniture for any gentleman's house. Although the most intelligent and informed patronage tended to buy Italian Old Masters (or more often copies of them), there was a fairly widespread encouragement of living painters (Pepys's patronage makes an interesting study of the way a rising official of the middle classes acquired his pictures). Artists in all branches could make some sort of a living, but as the richest demand was for Old Masters, the demand for contemporary work was only substantial enough financially to attract lesser artists, very often from abroad and particularly from the Low Countries. In England there was no established tradition of still-life, landscape, genre, or marine painting; into the gap flooded minor artists from across the seas, and the early history in England of these branches of

15. Francis Barlow. *Birds in a Landscape*, *c.*1680 (24½ by 28 in, 62·2 by 71·1 cm; Francis Tyrwhitt-Drake Collection)

painting looks like a provincial extension of Dutch art, reflecting a comfortable but uncritical taste, yet one which as it strengthened and refined through the first half of the century was to make possible the breeding of a truly native school. The names of Hondius, Wyck, Roestraaten, Heemskerck, and many others are now unknown outside specialist circles, but from them descend the great strains of English landscape, animal and genre painting. And some of the immigrant painters were of greater stature than they, and still fondly remembered. The Van de Veldes, father and son, switched side abruptly, and from painting the triumphs of the Dutch navies turned without heart-searching to the equally lively rendering of their

33

enemies' ships, the English; they were the best marine artists of the age in Europe, capturing with a fresh accuracy that was quite new the rolling, rhythmic balance between sea and ship and wind; their work has a sprightly free elegance which sometimes is subdued in their paintings but fully preserved in their drawings [13, 14]. One English-born artist exerts a perennial appeal, as naïve and basic as that of Aesop whom he illustrated: Francis Barlow. In landscape settings of a rather formalized Netherlandish kind, the birds and animals in his drawings and paintings are mounted with objective and careful skill. They have a sort of lumbering weight and presence; it is as though a taxidermist of genius, instead of working in the medium of the vitrines of a natural-history museum, had turned his hand to painting [15].

Hogarth

Hogarth used to be called the Father of English Painting, but it is a label that is only true if you take it to mean that he was the first in time of the great English-born painters of the eighteenth century. Though history in its deepening perspective has now revealed him, in the full European context, as the most important English painter of the century, the calibre of his greatness was far from recognized by his contemporaries in this country, and he had no artistic progeny here, no followers of any consequence to carry on and develop his style. In fact he spent his life in conflict with the fashionable taste of his time, embattled against the connoisseurs – a bitter struggle for any artist to undertake, for it was the connoisseurs who controlled, as far as painting was concerned, the artist's livelihood, by what they bought or did not buy.

The scale of values by which the eighteenth century assessed works of art was the natural and logical outcome of a classical and Mediterranean education. In literature, the highest possible form was held to be the grand epic, challenging comparison with Homer and with Virgil; so too, in painting, a truly major work could be nothing less than the visual equivalent of the epic, the history painting: the representation of some heroic scene from classical history or mythology. Only in this sort of art, it was felt, could the abilities of the artist be most fully extended, and the highest faculties of the spectator most meaningfully exercised. All other kinds of painting were, in comparison with history-painting, only minor ventures; painting, wrote the connoisseur John Elsum in 1703, 'is like Musick, best in Concert. History-Painting is that Concert, comprising all the other Parts of Painting, and the principal end of it is to move the Passions.' Any painter ambitious of greatness had therefore to answer this challenge, and the history of English painting for over a hundred years is strewn with their failures, interesting as corpses for academic dissection, impotent as corpses 'to move the Passions' of the modern onlooker. Yet the problem, for the painters who strove with it, was far from academic; with it was bound up the whole question of the honour of their art. At the beginning of the eighteenth century, the professional status of a painter was still uneasy; the Elizabethan Stow had stigmatized painting as 'base and mechanical, and a mere mestier of an Artificer and handy Craftsman', certainly no career for a gentleman, and much theoretical writing about painting after that was concerned with rehabilitation, intellectually and socially, of the artist. This explains Jonathan Richardson's pleasure when he was able to establish (to his own satisfaction at least) that Raphael was superior to Virgil, the argument being that the painter (of histories) had to have the same knowledge of art, science, and histories as did the writer, plus one talent that the writer did not have, that of the 'Curious Artificer'. Richardson wrote early in the century; his theories were vindicated by the career, writings, and to an extent, the practice, of Sir Joshua Reynolds – the pictures by which Reynolds succeeded were not strictly 'history-pictures'. And although artists were to be recognized, as it were, as worthy and fully-fledged members of society at last, the stickiness of the market in which they had to sell their most ambitious wares is best illustrated by the story of the patron who went to view Benjamin West's painting of *Pylades and Orestes*, yet did not buy it even though he liked it. Upon his son querying his decision against it, he said: 'You surely would not have me hang a modern English picture in my house, unless it were a portrait?' For the rich English patron, his education polished off by the Grand Tour, great Art was a monopoly of the Continent, and mainly of Italy.

The snobbery and quackery that this attitude could breed only too easily were a constant butt of Hogarth's satire; Hogarth's nationalistic fervour could indeed come close to chauvinism. Reynolds, in a self-portrait we shall consider later, is accompanied by a bust of Michelangelo; in Hogarth's self-portrait, the artist is accompanied into posterity by his dog, his palette (the tools of the trade, not mentioned in Reynolds's portrait), and by the works of Shakespeare, Milton, and – significantly – of Swift [16]. Yet Hogarth himself was not immune to the lure of the history-picture in the Continental

16. William Hogarth. *Self-Portrait*, 1745 (35½ by 27½ in, 90·2 by 69·9 cm; Tate Gallery, London)

manner; he was after all the son-in-law of Sir James Thornhill, the best English master of huge Baroque décor. Hogarth regarded himself as, among other things, the heir to the Grand Manner, and made various attempts in that manner. These are not, in fact, contemptible as contemporaries asserted; yet, while mostly worthy, respectable, and even, historically, of importance, they are boring. His genius was not for such generalized statements in an established tradition, but for a precise and lively comment on particular fact. If his work is uneven in quality throughout his career, its liveliness is never in doubt, served by a quick and deft command of his paint in which the heavy undulations of the Baroque break into the run and flicker of the Rococo. He loathed symmetry (beloved of contemporary neo-classic connoisseurs of the school of the Earl of Burlington), and put his faith in the 'beauty of a composed intricacy of form' that 'leads the eye a kind of chase', along a serpentine line through three dimensions – his famous S-line, the theory of which he developed in his book, *The Analysis of Beauty*. All his best work invites the eye to this kind of dance. It is there even in his straightforward head-and-shoulders portraits – which offer also a veracity and plainness new to English portraiture, if not generally a very searching characterization; it is there likewise in various degree in his earliest efforts at conversation-pieces, small-scale family groups, made in the seventeen-thirties, and especially it enlivens his series of pictorial satires.

The first of these famous series was *The Harlot's Progress* of 1731 (the originals were burnt in 1755), and the second, *The Rake's Progress*, finished by 1735 and now in Sir John Soane's Museum. Hogarth seems to have hit on the idea of these series by accident, but once conceived it was soon backed by a deliberate programme, the claims of which were stressed by his friend and sympathizer, the novelist Henry Fielding. The writer saw in Hogarth a great comic history painter, even as he held himself to be a serious comic-epic prose writer. 'The Epic, as well as the Drama,' wrote Fielding, 'is divided into Tragedy and Comedy'; the two are of equal intellectual stature. Hogarth's satires were not burlesques; besides being, in the formal sense, serious painting, they were also serious moral and social satires. He was entirely in key, if not with the patrons of high art, then with the moral and philanthropic mood of his age, as expressed in the life and work of such men as the Fieldings, Henry and his brother John, one of the first of the great Metropolitan magistrates. His art was, in the modern term, 'committed': a reflection, an interpretation, and a commentary on the social condition of his time. He found inspiration, not in other people's art (though he borrowed readily and without acknowledgement from a great variety of sources), but in life and nature on his doorstep and in

17. William Hogarth. *The Rake's Progress II: The Levee*, c.1732
(24½ by 29½ in, 62·2 by 74·9 cm; Sir John Soane's Museum, London)

the London streets: 'my Picture was my Stage, and men and women my actors, who were by means of certain actions and expressions to exhibit a dumb show.'

The Rake's Progress, like the other series, was made a commercial possibility by its widespread sale in engraved form (the paintings were basically only one stage towards the engravings, which perhaps partly accounts for their unevenness). In the first scene, Tom Rakewell enters unexpectedly, still a student, upon his inheritance. In the second scene, reproduced here [17], we see him at his morning levee as a sort of trainee man of the world, but beset already by money-sucking parasites. The ante-room beyond is full of vendors of personal finery; in the foreground the hero is surrounded by the necessary retainers of a young blood. His musician is thumping out *The*

18. William Hogarth. *The Marriage à la Mode II: Early in the Morning* (27 by 35 in, 68·6 by 88·9 cm; National Gallery, London)

Rape of the Sabines; crowded about him are a landscape gardener, a fencing master, quarterstaff instructor, and on the walls behind, evidence that one of those dealers in 'Old Masters' had already found an easy victim in the young man. The vanity and busy vapidness of Tom, still rather gauche, face advancing from brow to nose and retreating swift from nose to chin, are succinctly portrayed, and the crowd around sharply individualized (they are said to be all portraits – Dubois the fencing master was killed in a duel in 1734). With its parade of futile gesture and almost audible cacophony, the painting demonstrates the squandering of a young man's character before it is even formed. In the next four paintings the tempo speeds up: Tom is seen drunk, in poor shape, being robbed by girls in a brothel. Then he is arrested for debt; the situation is salvaged, by marriage with an aged decrepit heiress, only to be lost again in a

19. William Hogarth. *Lord George Graham in His Cabin*, *c*.1745
(25 by 27 in, 63·5 by 68·6 cm; National Maritime Museum, London)

gaming house, and thence to the Fleet prison, and the last terrible
view of Tom, naked and raving, in Bedlam. Such a moral tale was
not of course new in literature or even entirely so in painting, but it
lives by the brilliance of the painter's observation and improvisation,
and by a sort of counterpoint of visual, purely formal, elegance
against the harsh and often squalid subject-matter; this technique
was brought to its peak in *The Marriage à la Mode* in the National
Gallery [18].

In his early pictures, his characters sometimes teem in his inven-
tiveness almost to overcrowding, even in his straight conversation-
pieces. He abandoned these (they did not pay well for the labour
expended) and the *Lord George Graham in His Cabin* [19] painted
about 1745, probably in celebration of a successful naval action off
Ostend, is a late exercise in a genre he had virtually abandoned. It is

41

however one of his happiest portrait groups, the antithesis of a formal family portrait; even the sloping walls of the ship seem relaxed in easy pleasure. His exuberance is under perfect control; for once he uses an almost symmetrical composition, the figures grouped as on a stage, but surely in deliberate light mockery in honour of the comic opera, with the dogs taking the leading part, that seems to be in progress. The composition has in fact a fresh and haunting lilt and swing that is anchored firmly on the little upright, bewigged figure of the pugdog on the right. The noise – mercifully unheard – would be appalling; the visual rhythm is enchanting.

Five years before this, in 1740, Hogarth had painted his master-piece on the life-size scale – 'the portrait that I painted with most pleasure, and in which I particularly wished to excel, was that of Captain Coram for the Foundling Hospital' [20]. The sitter, a former captain in the Merchant Service, was a key figure in that moral, socially philanthropic movement with which Hogarth was in such sympathy. In 1738, Coram had founded the Foundling Hospi-tal, with which Hogarth was associated in a gesture which was characteristically both genuinely charitable and designed to adver-tise the arts (and himself). He gave his portrait of Coram to the Hospital, an example followed by other artists; these pictures were open for people to see, and in effect constituted the first public exhibition gallery of pictures in England. Hogarth's faith in his own contribution has been amply justified, and it still stands as one of the most remarkable European portraits of the eighteenth century. Designed as a set-piece in the grand manner, a formal portrait for the board room of a charitable institution, it is based in composition on a portrait by the French master of the court-portrait, Rigaud (a portrait which Hogarth knew by an engraving of it). But while enough of the conventional rhetoric – the pillar and drapery, the accumulation of furniture, and the deliberately self-conscious pose of the figure – have been retained to set the picture among its peers as a formal portrait, the whole conception has been subtly modulated to convey also the essential informality, the honesty both forth-right and unassuming of the seventy-year-old sea-captain. Bluff, gay, he sits there, a man happy in his duty, his legs scarcely long enough to reach the ground. It is, as it were, an aristocratic platitude entirely revitalized by its translation, with unerring sensibility, into middle-

20. William Hogarth. *Captain Thomas Coram*, 1740 (93 by 57 in,
236·2 by 144·8 cm; Thomas Coram Foundation for Children, London)

class terms. There are countless society portraits almost identical in pose and accessories, and giving the impression that their sitters are about to unburden themselves of an opening speech of unbearable tedium. If Coram were to open his mouth, it would be to comment – as he did at Dr Mead's table, on the toast to the Governors of the Foundling Hospital – hoping 'the new ones will be better than the last, who were rogues enough'. 'But these Governors,' said the startled Dr Mead, 'you don't suppose? . . .' 'I expect little better than the former.'

Eighteenth-Century Landscape

By the time of Hogarth's death in 1764, a new generation had already established itself in London, with a new kind of art and a new attitude to art. The foundation of the Royal Academy in 1769 gave artists, or at least those artists whom it accepted, a social and intellectual Establishment, with a constitution; a school; and an annual mart in which artists' wares could be displayed. It was not of course the first Academy of art in England, but none of the others had had royal patronage and, more important, none of them had lasted, split by the usual internecine jealousies to which artists seem particularly prone. The Royal Academy (though it had no dearth of jealousies) endured, and presently, in his famous *Discourses* delivered annually to the students, its President Sir Joshua Reynolds began to formulate its creed. Reynolds was not only the leading practitioner, but he was also, in a way unknown in English society hitherto, profoundly in harmony with the dominant artistic mood of the time and with its whole intellectual and social temper – the metropolitan culture whose centre was London. This however does not prove that he painted greater pictures than some others who stood more or less clear of the Academy mainstream. By 1750, a number of native-born artists were making very fair livings in branches other than the 'safe' one of portrait-painting. It was probably generally difficult to get started in such lines, and evidently impossible to interest certain patrons with Continental tastes at all; but nevertheless there were distinguished painters in landscape, sea-painting, and animal-painting, quite apart from Hogarth's innovation of satirical comic painting. For Englishmen it may be true that landscape and animal-painting, and to an extent sea-painting have always been best loved when they retain something of portraiture – *are* portraits, in fact, recognizable likenesses of their own

21. Samuel Scott. *A First-Rate Shortening Sail* (89 by 86 in, 226·1 by 218·4 cm; National Maritime Museum, London)

parks, houses, or towns, of their cities, of their ships or sea-battles. Even the ideal landscapes that they bought abroad were often souvenirs of a golden voyage of youth, echoes of Italy and a classical past – Claude and Gaspar Poussin.

The best landscapes painted in England at the close of the seventeenth and the beginning of the eighteenth centuries were certainly topographical in nature, by artists of Dutch or Flemish origin, and then most notably by Wootton and by George Lambert, a colleague and contemporary of Hogarth who on occasion could give an agreeable flavour of Gaspar Poussin, a touch of romance, to the portraits of his clients' English country houses. In marine-painting, the leading figure was Samuel Scott, also a contemporary of Hogarth, who began by painting in the manner of the Van de Veldes [21] (he owned many drawings by them, and his early pictures often get attributed to them), but who later switched to townscape, almost certainly in answer to a demand that had been created by yet another foreigner – Canaletto. It is tempting to consider Canaletto as an integral part of the English school; it is indeed almost justifiable to do so. His chief clients were almost all English (there are still more Canalettos in this country than anywhere else) and his unofficial but most effective sales-agent in Venice was the English Consul, Smith. His paintings were widely known here, brought back by young Englishmen as perfect souvenirs, before he himself came in 1746. He was in England for perhaps almost nine years – nearly as long as Holbein, almost exactly as long as Van Dyck. And he is at his best (though most of his English work unfortunately is not his best) the supreme example of the portrait painter of places, crystallizing an austere poetry out of topographical fact. The precision of his deep perspectives was pinpointed with the aid of a mechanical *camera*, but no such aid explains the luminous air that floods them, nor the living immediacy of his sense of place. The time is now; the salty winds crisp the water, and when you pass from the bland sunlight across the sharp edge of shadow it strikes cool. London has had no such painter before or since – Turner, Whistler, Monet, and many others found their own interpretations, but no one else saw it thus, in its rare moments of complete clarity, sharp as Venice [22–4].

It may be indeed that his eye, conditioned to the light of Venice, transposed it on to London, as later Dufy, once he had seen Mediterranean blues, managed to find them still when he returned to paler Channel waters. Scott, following close in Canaletto's footsteps in his views of London, caught perhaps more of the veil of moisture that is almost always in English skies. But Scott lacked the Venetian's spaciousness and the logic of his picture-making. Thus his views of the (now-covered) joining of the Fleet river with the Thames are at once a little shallow and a little congested, although, as in his

22. Antonio Canaletto. *Whitehall from Richmond House*, *c*.1747
(43 by 47 in, 109·2 by 119·4 cm; The Trustees of the
Goodwood Collection)

23. Detail from *Whitehall from Richmond House*

24. Detail from *Whitehall from Richmond House*

formula for indicating the ripple on the water's surface, he borrows straight from Canaletto.

In 1748, Scott was prospering, and moved from the artists' quarter in London out to the most fashionable village of Twickenham. Into a former house of his at Covent Garden there moved a young and promising Welsh painter, Richard Wilson. Wilson was then starting a career as portrait painter, but in the early fifties he was in Italy, and there changed to what was to prove his real subject – landscape. In this switch, he was probably primarily influenced, like Scott before him, by an Italian – Zuccarelli, who had had considerable success in London with his pretty, arcadian, and rather sugary Italian landscapes. In contrast, Wilson developed a stronger, more severe style, in which the classic inspiration of the two French masters of the Italian landscape, Claude and Gaspar Poussin, is very clear; as also, rather later, is that of the broad shimmering golden visions of the Dutchman, Cuyp.

The *Ruins of the 'Villa of Maecenas' at Tivoli* [25], painted probably in Italy just before his return to England about 1756 is a fine example of the 'ruin-scape'. The contemporary mood which they echoed is perhaps best indicated by a description of a composition by a young painter, Jonathan Skelton. Skelton was writing from Tivoli to his patron in England perhaps in the same year that Wilson painted this picture. Skelton's subject was the Grand Cascade of Tivoli –

On the right hand in the foreground is an aged Oak (as I think Mr Grey phrases it 'rearing his wanton Roots so high'); under it in a pensive contemplative Attitude an Old Man leaning on a Mossy Stone with a Book before him. On the left is the Temple of Concord half buried in Ruins, whose top is almost enveloped in lofty Pines, Cypresses, and Limes. To the right on the middle Ground is Coestus's Pyramidal Tomb, beyond grouping with these Ruins is the lofty Arched Temple of Peace. Behind all is a towering rocky Mountain in gloom which deprives our sight of the pleasing Skies; from the Mountain falls, now hid and then rising again, broad Cascades, whose general flow is the Line of Beauty; their last appearance is through the ruins of the Temple of Peace. One may draw many pleasing reflections from those venerable Relics of ancient Roman Grandeur composed in this manner: they show how Time erases everything, for those noble and immense Edifices were certainly (by their manner of building) intended to stand for ever.

This is redolent, as is, in its less complicated way, Wilson's canvas, of a cultivated elegiac melancholy; (Wilson himself, a blunt creature, was less articulate than Skelton; his verbal response to the equally well-known falls at Terni was confined, according to legend, to a brief but splendid and justly famous apostrophe: 'Well done water, by God!'). Yet in spite of his accord with a characteristic mood of his time, back in England Wilson was never a quick-fire success, probably because he was in a way too close to the style of the great landscapists whose inspiration he reflected and renewed – but, unlike them, he was British-born with a most British name, still a grave handicap as the story of West's non-buying patron indicates. Wilson's English work of the sixties and seventies, more various than is often thought, is at its best of a calm, sun-basking, poetic distinction; to the English landscape he transferred something of the miraculously lucid Roman light, in which objects in the countryside can

26. Richard Wilson. *Cader Idris: Llyn-Y-Cau*, *c.* 1770 (16 by 28 in, 40·6 by 71·1 cm; Collection of Lord Mostyn)

seem to group themselves consciously into picture, as though the Almighty Himself were a painter [26]. On other occasions Wilson found in the Welsh and in the English scene a radiant yet brooding tenderness, the placid mystery of wide stretches of water, over which the eye is drawn deep into the picture to the far haze on the horizon where sight seems to melt. Such is his vision of Hounslow Heath [27]. Sometimes he also made a bid to align his compositions with the classic example of Claude by peopling them with classic or mythological figures, but the figures tend to be essentially extraneous in a way they are not in Claude.

Sir George Beaumont, the doyen of grand British connoisseurs at the turn of the eighteenth century into the nineteenth, once contrasted Wilson with Gainsborough in Burkian terms: Wilson represented the 'Sublime', Gainsborough the 'Beautiful'. Hence in Beaumont's opinion

the superior popularity of Gainsborough cannot surprise us; since for one person capable of relishing the sublime, there are thousands who admire the rural and the beautiful, especially when set off by such fascinating spirit and splendour of colour as we see in the best works of Gainsborough.

25. Richard Wilson, '*Maecenas Villa at Tivoli*', *c.* 1756 (14¼ by 10 in, 35·61 by 25 cm; Tate Gallery, London)

27. Richard Wilson. *On Hounslow Heath*, c. 1770 (17¾ by 21¾ in, 45·4 by 55·3 cm; Tate Gallery, London)

For Beaumont, Wilson was of the greater intellectual and cultural calibre; the distinction between the painters reminds one of Milton's contrast of Ben Jonson's 'learned sock' with Shakespeare's 'native woodnotes wild'. But the most remarkable of Gainsborough's landscapes, inasmuch as the qualities of freshness and intuition are concerned, were probably unknown to Beaumont, and have in fact only found a full appreciation this century. These are his very early landscapes, painted in Suffolk about 1750; strictly they are not pure landscapes as they include portraits, but the synthesis of the two genres is so perfect that the pictures become portraits of more than a person – of a whole way of life, of a country gentry blooming modestly and naturally among their woods and fields, their parks and lakes [28]. The directness of characterization is so straightforward as to seem almost naïve – as if a brilliant doll-maker had learnt from

28. Thomas Gainsborough. *Sportsman with Two Dogs in a Landscape*
c. 1755 (30 by 25½ in, 76·2 by 64·8 cm; Collection of the
Earl of Inchcape)

Watteau (whose influence is in fact traceable in some of these paintings). The light on land and tree and water has a rainwashed brilliance,
and a strange tension of stillness – sometimes it is almost a thunder-
light.

In his later pure landscapes, the woodenness melts under the
brush of a painter who loved the radiant shimmering fluency of his
medium as perhaps no other English painter has ever done. Reynolds praised in Gainsborough 'his manner of forming all the parts

29. Thomas Gainsborough. Detail from *The Market Cart*, 1786
(72½ by 60¼ in, 184·2 by 153 cm; Tate Gallery, London)

of his picture together; the whole going on at the same time, in the same manner as nature creates her works'. In one of the most famous of his late landscapes, *The Market Cart* [29], painted two years before he died, this 'natural' mastery is combined with an equally magnificent and fully conscious mastery of formal composition; it is painted by a man who had studied Ruysdael profoundly and learnt much from him, but the knowledge is applied direct to the English landscape, and the result retains the spontaneity of first vision – the movement of the girls in the cart and of the horse not frozen, but transposed into the movement of the brush. This is the 'rural and the beautiful' at its greatest; in comparison, Wilson's views of the 'sublime', noble though they are, seem a little contrived, deliberately picturesque – scenic.

Wright of Derby and George Stubbs

Wilson and Gainsborough form the two main peaks in eighteenth-century landscape painting. But landscape was not the only alternative to portrait painting. (To Gainsborough's portraits I shall come back later.) Quite apart from the elusive will-o'-the-wisp of history-painting, there was by now a fairly rewarding market for flower-pieces, still-lifes, genre pieces (scenes from contemporary life, the rustic farmyard anecdotes of which Morland was the finest practitioner; scenes from plays and so on). But for such paintings the leading connoisseurs still went to foreign sources, and it was not the leaders of taste who bought the English ones, but a humbler, more bourgeois clientele, and no major English talent was strongly enough impelled to devote himself mainly to such themes. There is no English counterpart to Chardin.

A most interesting figure, though not a great genius, was however Joseph Wright of Derby, an able enough painter with a remarkable range of interests. He was conventionally London-trained (like Reynolds, under the society portrait painter Thomas Hudson) in portraiture, and he made the, by then, conventionally necessary trip to Italy, but it was to his native Midlands that he returned in the end. In his work there comes through something of the hard-headed, practical yet romantic excitement of the dawn of the Industrial Revolution. He saw the world in a forced and sharpening light – sometimes artificial, the mill-windows brilliant in the night, faces caught in the circle of the lamp, or the red glow of an iron forge, casting monstrous shadows. This was an old trick – deriving from Caravaggio and the Dutch candlelight painters – but with it Wright brought out a sense of exploration and exploitation – scientific, intellectual, and commercial, the spirit of the Midlands of his time. His patrons were men like the industrialist Arkwright of the spinning

30. Joseph Wright of Derby. *Experiment on a Bird in the Air-Pump*, c. 1768 (72 by 96 in, 182·9 by 243·9 cm; Tate Gallery, London)

jenny, and Dr Priestley, the poetic seer of the new science (both of whom he painted).

The *Experiment on a Bird in the Air-Pump* [30], painted in 1768, is perhaps his masterpiece. Air-pumps were in considerable production in the Midlands at the time, but this is not merely an excellently painted and composed study of a scientific experiment. It is raised to the pitch of a true and moving drama of life, not only by the heightening of mood by the dramatic lighting or the subtly differentiated characterization of the participants, but by the tender yet unsentimental exploration of a human situation. The bird in the globe will die, as the vacuum is created in it; the elder girl on the right, sentimental in herself but unsentimentally drawn, cannot bear the idea and hides her face in her hands, while the younger one, though half-turned away also, looks up still to the bird with a marvellous and marvelling expression in which curiosity is just overcoming fear and pity. The haloed moon, on the edge of cloud, seen through the window on the right, adds another dimension of weirdness and mystery. (Wright painted too some scenes that could serve as illustrations to the Gothick novels, like Mrs Radcliffe's, of moonlight, passion, and ruins.)

This is a picture that exists on many levels, and one that comes closer to the complex effect that classical or mythological history-painters were aiming at than did any perhaps of the strictly history-paintings produced at the time. But, as it was not expressed in terms of the classical culture of the age, Wright's subject pictures were for long not given their due. He himself stood apart from that culture; although he early became an Associate of the Royal Academy, he soon quarrelled with it.

George Stubbs presents in some ways a similar case: he never became a full member of the Royal Academy and his 'grading' was a low one in terms of subject-matter. He was, for his contemporaries, a mere horse-painter. In the last few years he has been much studied, and his reassessment has lifted him to the level of the greatest of his time, the peer in his very different way of Reynolds and Gainsborough. His life has been fairly described as heroic. The son of a Liverpool currier, he supported himself at the beginning of his career in northern England by painting portraits, but at the same time started in on his study of anatomy, animal and human, that was to prove not only vitally important to his art but also a new contribution to science. Stubbs was one of the great English empiricists; when he went to Rome about the age of thirty, it was – so he is reported by a contemporary – 'to convince himself that nature was and is always superior to art whether Greek or Roman – and having received this conviction he immediately resolved upon returning'. Soon afterwards occurred the episode that has most fascinated and astonished the imagination of posterity: he took a farm-house in Lincolnshire and in it, over eighteen months, he grappled with the anatomy of the horse. His models were the decaying carcasses of horses, which he gradually stripped down, recording each revelation of anatomy in precise and scientific drawing. The result was his book *The Anatomy of the Horse*, a pioneering work both in science and in art.

31. George Stubbs. *Mares and Foals*, 1762 (40 by 75 in,

All his painting is based on knowledge drawn from tenacious and ruthless study, ordered by a most precise observation and scrupulous composition. In the seventies, his scientific interests widened from anatomy to chemistry, and helped by Wedgwood, the enlightened founder of the great pottery firm, he experimented in enamel painting. But his associations with high fashion in culture (one is

(101·6 by 190·5 cm; The Earl Fitzwilliam)

almost tempted to write, unfairly, *haute couture*) were always cool; he had ambitions to succeed as portrait painter and as history painter which were never fulfilled, and he died in old age far from well off. His true and great originality was not on conventional lines, and could not be grasped by contemporary taste. His is a more austere, more purely pictorial, more naked poetry than that of any

32. George Stubbs. Detail from *The Hambletonian*, 1799 or 1800
(The Viscountess Bury)

other English painter, and can at its best attain a still, self-sufficient
monumentality – most remarkably perhaps in his friezes of horses
[31] or in the famous life-size painting of the race-horse Hambletonian with its groom [32]. His portrait, *A Lady and Gentleman in
a Carriage* [33], may seem at first sight no more than another, ad-
mittedly fine, example of the outdoor conversation piece, often
involving animals, that was popular at the time. But comparison
with an excellent but conventional example of one of these underlines Stubbs's exceptional qualities.

Take for example Johann Zoffany's *Lord Willoughby de Broke and
Family* [34]. Zoffany was a German-born painter with Italian experience, a founder-member of the Royal Academy, who specialized
in England in the conversation piece, whether of actors in scenes
from stage-plays (he was a friend of Garrick) or straightforward

family groups. While lacking the satiric verve of Hogarth, he was of an enviable and delightful professional ability, yet his group, compared with Stubbs's, remains only on the level of anecdotery; all is affection, good humour, romp, and charm, but it is a stage grouping (although much more successful purely as composition than most of Zoffany's works) rather than a fused pictorial unity. It is an artistic contrivance, lacking what might be called artistic inevitability. In contrast the silence of the Stubbs is superb. Here there is no anecdotal interest; nothing is forced and the picture is balanced as delicately as scales on the central vertical of the poplars in the background. The painting of the intricacies of the carriage is not a mere *tour de force* of painstaking realism, but is subordinate to the movement of the picture: the two figures, leaning slightly in the seat, echo the outward tilt of the wheels. The magnificent sleek black animals balance the human figures and the carriage; everything is characterized with a sort of detached, precise passion and informed by an exact

33. George Stubbs. *A Lady and Gentleman in a Carriage*, 1787 (32½ by 40 in, 82·6 by 101·6 cm; National Gallery, London)

34. Johann Zoffany. *John Peyto, Fourteenth Baron Willoughby de Broke, and Louisa, his wife,* c.1770 (39½ by 49½ in, 100·3 by 125·7 cm; Collection of Lord Willoughby de Broke)

knowledge of the physical structure of each object. Stubbs's hard-won first-hand experience of anatomy is reflected in his pictures; they too have a rigorous essential anatomy, an organic structure behind them that gives them a logic unmatched in English painting. In the Lincolnshire farm-house he had served an apprenticeship similar in kind though not in method to that of the apprentice in an Italian painter's workshop in the Renaissance, and on such a discipline rests the unfumbling classic sureness of his touch and of his art of picture-building.

Conversation Pieces

About 1725, a new kind of English painting had begun to crystallize in a formula, which with many variations was to remain popular throughout the eighteenth century; it is indeed now perhaps the most immediately captivating and most satisfactorily English of all kinds of painting in the period: the Conversation Piece, a small-scale group portrait of two or generally more people about their normal occasions – if still generally polite occasions, still most refreshingly normal in contradistinction to the apotheosis attempted by most formal society portraiture before. And they are portraits not merely of people but of people in specific settings – in a room in their house, surrounded by their furniture, pictures, and books; or in the grounds of their houses, often with animals and especially of course with horses. We have glimpsed some of them in the preceding pages, and it is time to consider them for themselves. In them art relaxes, and they reflect a stable, unquestioning, and unquestionable social order, the prosperity and peace of the middle years of the Hanoverian era. It is of course a strictly selective view of that society; for other aspects one need only turn to Fielding's novels or to Hogarth's satirical paintings, but at its best it records its subjects from its selected angle with as much veracity as does the print of *Gin Lane* – Hogarth was of course the supreme master of both views.

It is not court-art; George II may have sat to Hogarth, and George III, frequently, to Zoffany, but Zoffany's pictures of George III's family are a vivid illustration of the completed domestication of royalty into middle-class constitutional monarchy. It is impossible to imagine any of the Stuarts shown seated at their dressing table as Zoffany painted Queen Charlotte (though very fully dressed of course).

It was not an English invention, but really a Dutch one, by

35. Arthur Devis. *William Atherton and His Wife, Lucy, c.* 1745–7
(36 by 50 in, 91·4 by 127 cm; Walker Art Gallery, Liverpool)

painters such as de Hooch and Steen, in certain of their pictures in
which one cannot always be sure whether the subject is dramatic
domestic genre or a family group. Hogarth, as we have seen in his
portrait of the admiral in his cabin [19] loved also to inject a dramatic content into his conventional pieces, and so too did Zoffany.
Zoffany was in fact the popularizer of an extension of the conversation piece, the painting of scenes from plays; he painted Garrick
thus in character in many plays, and was surely an important agent
in that actor's highly developed personal publicity machine. And
even though Zoffany, in his cosy, meticulously detailed family
groups, is the most thoroughly domestic of the best painters of conversation pieces (in his interiors you see sometimes a coal fire
burning in the grate, and his carpets are all but Victorian in their
florid warmth), he always intensifies them with an emphasis of
grouping and gesture that belongs to the stage. He is lively, if a
little obvious in characterization (though marvellous on the subject

of the high plain face of the British matron); the Willoughby de Broke family [34] shows him at his anecdotal best, and it was perhaps unfair to compare this unpretentious delight with the majesty of Stubbs.

A great many hands' turned their attention at times to the conversation piece, including (besides Hogarth) Gainsborough, Stubbs, and even Reynolds (though very rarely; when rashly young and in Rome, he painted unexpectedly some pure caricature conversations): these painters we consider elsewhere. Zoffany is not the quintessentially English conversation-piece painter; his mirror has if not a German, then surely a Hanoverian, tint in its reflection, not so much comfortable as *gemütlich*. After Hogarth, the pure English master was a minor but now very popular painter, Arthur Devis. He was a provincial (Walpole found his gaucherie offensive) working mainly in the north, and a specialist in the genre. He hardly ever attempts to enliven his pictures by incident: they are rather straightforward group portraits (often with the air of a package deal), their subjects not so much posing as frankly posed, like dolls, by the painter. They are angular, often of a mysterious silvery tonality, in which the figures cast no shadow [35]; brimming with silence, they are yet more suggestive of past music, of time arrested, than any of the musical groups, bristling with instruments, that Zoffany loved to accumulate.

Reynolds

Hogarth, Wright, Stubbs – all artists wrongly estimated or under-estimated by their contemporaries – are now revealed stripped of the conventions of their times in what seems a truer perspective. In contrast, consider now the artist who was in full accord with his times and honoured by them as no English artist had been honoured before – Sir Joshua Reynolds. Unlike Stubbs, he has at present somewhat depreciated, if you consider him purely as artist; yet, as a sort of historical monument, as an embodiment of his age, he still stands upon his eminence, central and commanding and admirable in our eyes. However much one may probe his weaknesses, however much his work may seem, in the last analysis, to lack that urgency that lifts the heart, one cannot but more admire, the more one studies his work.

Unlike Stubbs or Wright, or even Gainsborough, he seems to have had all the advantages. Socially he was impeccably successful, consorting as respectful equal not only with the aristocracy of birth but with the still fabulous aristocracy of merit of that remarkable age: the intimate of Dr Johnson and of Burke, the befriender of Goldsmith. In his own sphere, the head of the profession: first President, and in large part begetter, of the Royal Academy, knight and an honorary Doctor of the University of Oxford. He was prosperous to a reasonable affluence; he was even successful as a man of letters, a theorist, able to support his practice with a reasoned and general philosophy nobly set out in a prose not unworthy of a friend of Johnson; Reynolds, amongst so many other things, made art-criticism respectable in England. Moreover personally he had great dignity, charm and urbanity.

Yet he was not born to most of these advantages; in his ambition and by his own capacity he created them, and his triumph is that of a

36. Thomas Hudson. *Marquis Townshend*, 1759 (49½ by 39 in.
125·7 by 99·1 cm; formerly in the Townshend Collection)

remarkable but not intrinsically outstanding ability developed to its
utmost by hard work and persistence and intelligence, and fired by
an unfailing devotion to the art which he served. His training was
orthodox enough, under the best master of society portraiture as it
was then understood, Thomas Hudson. But there was perhaps only
one lesson relevant to Reynolds's particular talent that Hudson
could have taught him, and that lesson unfortunately Reynolds did
not heed: the necessity of a sound technique in painting (many of

37. Allan Ramsay. *The Artist's Wife*, *c.* 1755 (29¼ by 24⅜ in, 74·3 by 61·9 cm; National Gallery of Scotland, Edinburgh)

Reynolds's paintings are now but ghosts of their original selves, owing to his irresponsible experimentation with techniques). To understand the extent of the revolution that Reynolds was to bring about, a word on the situation that he found upon his arrival on the scene in the seventeen-forties is necessary. It was, in brief, a *status quo*; society portraiture had become a monotonous repetition of the same theme with only the most limited of variations permissible. According to the formula, the sitter was to be posed centrally, with the background (curtain, pillar, chair, perhaps a hint of landscape) disposed like a backdrop behind; normally the head was done by the master, the body by a pupil or 'drapery assistant' who might serve several painters. Pose and expression, even the features themselves, tended to be regulated to a standard of polite and inexpressive elegance; the portraits told little about their subjects other than that they were that sort of people who had their portraits painted – they certainly gave nothing away beyond the summary description of the features. They were effigies; life has departed [36].

Before Reynolds there were certain stirrings of revolt. Allan Ramsay, whose early portraits of the forties can be sometimes confused with those by Hudson (although Ramsay had a lightness of touch and a flexibility unknown to Hudson), was capable of far subtler variations than most. In some ways he even forestalled Reynolds, and in his best later work (sometimes influenced by Reynolds's example) he rivalled him. Indeed, in his later portraits, in one aspect, compared with the earlier works of Reynolds, he could be superior to the younger man. Horace Walpole remarked – 'Mr Reynolds seldom succeeds in women, Mr Ramsay is formed to paint them.' (The criticism does not apply by any means to some of Reynolds's later female portraits.) That was in 1759; Ramsay's portrait of his wife [37] dates from about that time. It is a silvery, cool-hued picture of the most elegant informality, with a conviction of live, easy intimacy that is a world away from Hudson and his school, and which, in simplicity, in warmth perhaps of discreet affection, is beyond the range of anything Reynolds ever painted. But a few years after this Ramsay found royal favour (almost the one worldly blessing denied to Reynolds), and the last twenty years of his life were spent in agreeable idleness, his main painting concern being the supervision of the production of royal state-portraits by assistants.

The more complex of Ramsay's portraits, however, occur relatively rarely in his work, and the revolution which they foreshadow was only realized by Reynolds. It was Reynolds who insisted in his practice that a portrait could and should be also a full, complex work of art on many levels; he conceived his portraits in terms of history-painting. Each fresh sitter was not just a physical fact to be recorded, but rather a story to be told (or sometimes, one suspects, a myth to be created). His people are no longer static, but caught between this

71

movement and the next, between one moment and the next. Their minds and bodies exist on the brink of various possibilities, and they are essentially involved in the weather of life [38, 39]. Sometimes they seem like actors, pausing in soliloquy. Reynolds was indeed a consummate producer of characters (whether they bore much resemblance to the originals, the raw stuff from which they were created, is another, academic, matter; in point of fact, the catching of a convincing likeness was not his forte), and his production methods reward investigation. For them he called upon the full repertoire of the Old Masters; in Italy, as a young man, he had studied the old masters of all schools, not so that he could ape their individual works, but in order to win a similar mastery of the effect which they knew how to achieve: to rival them in their own language but not to pastiche them. In the building up of the picture in light and shade, his handling of the intrinsic drama of a composition, he also paid homage to Rembrandt. In the actual design, he had the whole Italian school as an inexhaustible well to draw upon. In his conception of the grand, the heroic, the sublime, he came more and more to invoke the spirit of Michelangelo. But all these contributions would have availed nothing – would on the contrary have been disastrous – if he had not possessed, in the first place, a mental and visual digestive ability of amazing capacity, and, secondly, a beautifully just feeling for composition. As it was, by his example he established English portraiture as a branch of painting of a similar kind to, and comparable with, the work of the Old Masters.

In fact he was avowedly what is called an eclectic, but there is a case for eclecticism. One of the primary requisites 'in our *Poet*, or Maker' (this is Ben Jonson, writing a century and a half earlier) 'is Imitation, to be able to convert the substance, or Riches of another *Poet*, to his own use. . . . Not to imitate servilely; but to draw forth out of the best and choicest of flowers, with the Bee and turn all into Honey.' This is a classic statement of the academic case; the danger is of course that originality may be underestimated (as it was by Reynolds) and that students following in the tradition may become paralysed by dependence on authority and dogma.

38. Sir Joshua Reynolds. Detail from *General Tarleton*, 1782 (National Gallery, London)

39. Sir Joshua Reynolds. *Lady Cockburn and Her Three Eldest Sons*, 1773 (55¾ by 44½ in, 141·6 by 113 cm; National Gallery, London)

It may be asked why, if Reynolds thought the greatest achievement in painting to be history-painting, he did not apply himself to it. He did, but not as his means of livelihood, because he could not have lived off it; in his practice but not in his theory (in his *Discourses*), he admitted that the traditional history-picture was no longer historically valid for his times; his solution, in marrying the history-picture to the portrait, was a brilliant and most English compromise; none of his history-pictures, the *Death of Dido* and all

40. Sir Joshua Reynolds. *Colonel St Leger*, 1778 (94 by 58½ in,
238·8 by 148·6 cm; National Trust, Waddesdon Manor)

41. Sir Joshua Reynolds. *Self-Portrait*, *c.*1773 (50 by 40 in, 127 by 101·7 cm; Royal Academy of Arts, London)

the many others, is in fact as satisfactory, nor 'works' as well as any of his finest portraits.

In the second example of his work reproduced here, the *Lady Cockburn and Her Three Eldest Sons* [39], his production methods can be studied in depth. The poses stir memories of the Caracci and of Rubens, the sumptuous red hangings echo Van Dyck, and the conception of the figure, the theme, has been related to the popular

Italian subject of Charity, and is perhaps traceable back to Michelangelo. As if this were not enough for undertones and overtones, when the picture was engraved it was titled, not with the sitter's name (which was Augusta Ann) but as *Cornelia and her children*, Cornelia being the mother of the Roman heroes, the Gracchi. (The brilliant macaw whose reds so boldly come to near-clash with those of the draperies has a more simple explanation, being a studio prop of Reynolds's that used to perch alarmingly on visitors' shoulders.) The picture is ably, even nobly realized, and much of its high cultural implications would have been recognizable by (or explainable to) the sitter and client, flattering her further by setting her so firmly among the classics; yet the taste of more recent times may well be jarred by something in this picture that seems close to affectation. It is in a key, a mode of sentiment, with which most of us are no longer in tune. And it is probably true to say that Reynolds was, in this case, exaggerating somewhat; it comes from his most classicizing period, the seventies, when he was striving to make his pictures as rich as possible. It is very much a 'public' picture, painted with exhibition specifically in mind in the newly founded artists' display ground at the Academy (it was shown there in 1774), and designed to compel the spectators' attention to itself, to the detraction of the works of his rivals.

Later, he was at his best in simpler compositions, though behind them there lies an ever-increasing experience and knowledge. Such is the whole-length portrait of *Colonel St Leger* [40] of 1778, a relatively simple but immensely subtle and fluent study against the ominous sky: a martial portrait, yet of extraordinary relaxation and breeding, balanced as lightly and crisply as a hair-spring. Surely few people can resist the sheer pleasure of this sort of Reynolds, and it may remind one of a remark he made in his apprentice days when writing home about his painting – 'While I am doing this I am the happiest creature in the world.'

The *Self-Portrait* [41] on the other hand speaks admirably and eloquently of the high seriousness of the great artist; he appears not as mere painter, but as the official representative of Art. Wearing his D.C.L. gown with senatorial dignity that recalls Titian, accompanied by a bust of Michelangelo, and enhanced by a mystery of light out of darkness that certainly owes much to Rembrandt, he presents himself nevertheless – with full confidence but not in arrogance – in

42. Sir Joshua Reynolds. *Lord Heathfield*, 1787 (56 by 44¾ in, 142·2 by 113·7 cm; National Gallery, London)

that superb decorum which was one of his characteristics. Compared with Rembrandt, it lacks inwardness and depth, and that magical fusion of flesh and spirit of the Dutchman's late self-portraits. But if it be true that Reynolds was not great among the greatest as was Rembrandt, nevertheless this noble portrait is of very high order, and expresses the best and most serious in its painter. For all his theory, he was ultimately an English empiricist, resting secure on the proven and individual fact – the individual presence of each fresh sitter whence, each time, a fresh start had to be made.

Gainsborough's Portraits

Thomas Gainsborough was Reynolds's rival and almost exact contemporary. He was also his most exact opposite, although the often-made contention that neither influenced the other in their painting is over-stated: Gainsborough surely owed much to the immense widening of scope that Reynolds's 'damned Variousness' had created for the portrait-painter, while pictures like Reynolds's *Colonel Coussmaker* (in New York) would never have had quite that fluent grace, I suspect, if he had never known Gainsborough's later work. I have already touched upon Gainsborough's early portraiture – that mingling of portraiture and landscape which he abandoned when he left Suffolk, about 1760, for the more sophisticated clientele of Bath. There he, as Reynolds had before him, turned to the Old Masters but primarily to only one of them, and not to an Italian (he never visited Italy) – but to Van Dyck. To this study he brought an innate genius for drawing that Reynolds never possessed, and a sensuous delight in colour and movement that seems at times to amount almost to intoxication with them. No other painter has thus caught, at his best, the essence of silks and lace in motion, nor the tremulous flicker of an eyelash. In contrast to Reynolds's, the essence of his genius was intuitive, and he profits far less from commentary; his art develops freely according to his own genius, the touch of the brush getting ever lighter, the atmosphere ever more aerial. To appreciate one of his great masterpieces, one does not need to have the likeness of his mood with that of Watteau, or the hint of *chinoiserie* in the delicately absurd hat, harped upon over much; one merely needs eyes to see with and enough life left to fall in love. Gainsborough is the purest lyricist of our painters; Reynolds the master of the epic style.

This portrait of *Lady Howe* [43, 44] was painted fairly early in his

43. Thomas Gainsborough. *Mary, Countess Howe, c.* 1765
(96 by 90 in, 243·8 by 228·6 cm; Iveagh Bequest, Kenwood)

44. Detail from *Mary, Countess Howe*

Bath period, about 1765; that is at a time when he had achieved a remarkable balance between the demands of the almost liquid urgency of his style and those of the necessity of combining with it a record of the minute detail that fixed the likeness of his subject. In his later style – the famous *Morning Walk* [frontispiece and 45] in the National Gallery is one of the finest examples of it – the sitters seem to merge one into another as though faces in a happy dream.

45. Thomas Gainsborough. *The Morning Walk*, *c*.1785 (93 by 70½ in,
236·2 by 179·1 cm; National Gallery, London)

Romney

The third of the great names of the late eighteenth century, whose works became so desirable to American millionaires in the early part of the twentieth century, was George Romney. His portraits have been much misunderstood, and he is in one sense the purest classicist of all the portrait-painters of his time: classical statuary inspired both the broad planes of his draperies, and the generalized serenity of his likenesses. At his worst he comes curiously close to the empty and hygienic handsomeness of Hollywood stars of the thirties, with a corresponding banality of sentiment. But at his best, as in his portraits of young English aristocrats poised on the brink of manhood (even if sometimes like Narcissus over the pool) he is a master of inexpressive elegance. Recently too, attention has revived in another aspect of his work, his attempt also to paint expression, the expressions of the mind. The rather unjustly notorious sequence of portraits of Lady Hamilton posing are part of this attempt; another part, his pen-and-ink studies for great, almost entirely unrealized 'historical' paintings, reflects an international obsession with the study of the 'elemental passions'. They are in fact strongly influenced by the work of Fuseli, the German-Swiss painter nurtured in the heart of the *Sturm ünd Drang* movement. Fuseli was an immensely learned artist, a true art-historian, but he applied his learning to the realization of the irrational in images of distortion and fantasy that have quickened anew in a century haunted by the sub-conscious. But Fuseli's technique in paint fell short of the originality of his vision, so that most of his work is now interesting more as documentary than as vital art; the true master of that other world of vision and imagination was to be Blake.

Romanticism

Towards the close of the eighteenth century, all over Europe, the tensions that had gradually built up behind the decorous, bewigged façade of the Age of Reason reached breaking point, and burst in revolution. The most violent manifestation was of course the French Revolution, followed by the wars that burned intermittently through Europe for the next twenty years. But this was too a period of less bloodily violent yet equally far-reaching revolutions in other spheres – in industry and commerce, the Industrial Revolution – that accelerated the change in social life to a remarkable pitch. And in art likewise, the Romantic Revolution.

Romanticism perennially escapes definition – it has so many aspects, some of which can be discerned in the most classical of classic art. As its most perspicacious commentator, Baudelaire, observed: 'Romanticism is precisely situated neither in choice of subjects nor in exact truth, but in a mode of feeling.' In fact, however elusive its definition may be, it is obvious beyond doubt that there was a fundamental shift in the nature of artistic expression at the time, and Baudelaire's remark at least points to the most important quality of this shift: the motive force consciously becomes emotion rather than reason. This does not, as is sometimes suggested, mean that reason was necessarily thrown overboard, but the irrational was acknowledged as at least as important as the rational. This helps one to understand a seeming paradox in much romantic art, when it seems to possess both near- and far-sight. Reynolds, writing in his *Discourses*, described 'the disposition to abstractions, to generalizing and classification' as 'the great glory of the human mind'; this remark provoked anathema from Blake in the margins of his copy of Reynolds's work: 'To Generalize is to be an Idiot; to particularize is the alone Distinction of Merit.' Again and again one finds the romantic artist dwelling, doting, on the particular, the detail, the minute – as Constable, for example, in his meticulously observed portraits of individual trees – yet the intensity of such contemplation finds in the exact detail intimations of a larger order, even of immortality. 'To see a World in a Grain of Sand, and a Heaven in a Wild Flower'. In the eighteenth century, the mean – the scale – had been set by the human figure, particularly in England, and the most significant art perhaps had been the portraiture of men and women. For the Romantics, the scale became superhuman; the scope of the body could not contain human passion, and it found its expression in all nature. An early critic of Turner, in 1799, was on the mark: 'Turner's views are not mere ordinary transcripts of nature; he always throws some peculiar and striking *character* into the scene he represents.' The sea in storm and calm, the vast movement of sky and cloud just as the dewdrop shining on the leaf, all become the expression, the symbols even, of man's desires and sorrows and doubts. The finite is only the microcosm of the infinite; a pool of rainwater after a shower postulates the whole sky, and heaven itself.

One danger is of course, once the human scale is abandoned, that all proportion may be lost. Blake, walking a tight-rope in mid-air among his teeming visions and with the hard earth beneath, crazy as a saint, sometimes seems to have lost all sense of proportion (without which one cannot communicate one's vision to other mortals). The true balance was held by Constable. (He, it is said, only met Blake once, when Blake was roused to enthusiasm by his drawings, crying: 'Why, this is not drawing, but *inspiration*!' – to which Constable replied: 'I never knew it before; I meant it for drawing.') Constable indeed, who is on record as saying that for him feeling was only another word for painting, also said: 'In such an age as this, painting should be *understood*, not looked on with blind wonder, nor considered only as a poetic inspiration, but as a pursuit, *legitimate*, *scientific*, and *mechanical*.'

But the wonder was certainly there: no blind rapture, but a passionate scrutiny, seeking the exact lineaments even of the infinite, that favourite romantic aspiration. 'Cursed be the picture that shows nothing beyond the finite,' wrote Delacroix, 'the merit of a picture is the indefinable; precisely that which escapes precision.' To achieve which one must proceed with almost surgical subtlety: one thinks of the earth melting into the colours of the prism, into light, in Turner's visions.

Romanticism was a European movement in art, but in it for the first time for centuries, with Constable and Turner especially, and with Lawrence in his manner, English artists led the way. But before coming to these great figures, we must glance, though only briefly, at a peculiarly English achievement that was to prove particularly congenial to the romantic search: the work of the watercolourists.

The Watercolour

Watercolour, so swift to use, so delicate, so portable, and so comparatively ephemeral compared with the solid painting of oil colours, is especially suited to catch just those ephemeral effects in nature in which the Romantics were so fascinated. Through the eighteenth century the medium became popular and widespread, but to begin with was used mainly for topographical purposes: to take the portrait, to make a record of a particular place – a patron's house, a special view. They were also mostly more tinted drawings than paintings; colour was subordinate, and generally from a very limited palette, often almost monochrome, used as a wash to give substance and relief to the line. With the work of Paul Sandby however, though he was trained as a strict record-taking topographer, a far greater vivacity and richness was introduced, and colour becomes no longer a mere fill-in – Sandby drew often not with the pencil, but with the brush.

The contribution of Francis Towne is a most individual variation on what might be called the opposite tradition in watercolour to that practised by Sandby: the counterpart of ideal landscape painting in oils, an interpretation, in poetic, elegiac terms rather than those of strict topography. In such watercolours the traveller recorded the picturesque wherever he came across it. The most influential document to tune English sensibilities to landscape for its own self was Thomson's famous poem *The Seasons*; as early as 1726, in his preface to *Winter*, he locates the poet's delight as in 'the wild, romantic country'. Writing in 1782 (the year after the drawing by Towne reproduced here [46] was made), the critic Warton indicated which aspects of nature had by then proved to be of particular appeal:

The *Seasons* of Thomson have been very instrumental in diffusing a general taste for the beauties of *nature* and *landscape*. It is only within a

46. Francis Towne. *Source of the Aveyron*, 1781 (16¾ by 12¼ in,
42·5 by 31·1 cm; Victoria and Albert Museum, London)

few years that the picturesque scenes of our own country, our lakes, mountains, cascades, caverns, and castles have been visited and described...

In his choice of wild mountain scenery for subject, then, Towne was typical of many watercolourists of his time; it is a fascination of course that was intensified in the generation of the Lakeist poets, and one that still has not lost its force. The manner of his description is however very personal; though the outlines are lucidly traced in the topographical manner, and the colour is a little flat and pale, the generalization of the natural forms into what, so it appears to modern eyes, is close to an abstract pattern, is unlike that of any other artist of the time, and achieves something of the strange visionary quality of Blake's world. A primeval world of a frozen yet fluid geometry is composed in a beautiful balance of broad contrasting tones; no other painter has succeeded in suggesting the *movement* of a glacier beneath its monumental seeming-immobility.

The enlargement of the possibilities of the medium that the work of Sandby and of Towne indicates are considerable, but less fundamental than that to which Sandby's contemporary, Alexander Cozens, and his son J. R. Cozens, pointed in their practice. The elder Cozens, in a work first published in 1759 as *An Essay to facilitate the invention of Landskips*, suggests an entirely new freedom. While on the one hand sensitive to the particular atmosphere of a particular time of day or effect of weather (noting occasionally on his drawings, much as Constable was to do later, comments such as 'before rain', or 'intermixture of clouds with the landscape'), he already is concerned with another approach typical of romantic landscape, by which it can become almost pure invention of the painter, a subjective mood manifested in rocks and trees, in sky and cloud and shadow. He was the inventor of the notorious 'blottesques'; free compositions made by elaborating designs from a spatter of blots and dashes in Indian ink thrown on the paper. Here we have the principle of accident and intuition introduced into English art (it goes a long way back, at least to Leonardo), and another principle which was to be formally set out by the connoisseur Richard Payne Knight in the nineties: that what moves us in a work of art is not the subject-matter, objective qualities in the thing seen, so much as 'light, variously gradated and modified' and the subjective

47. Alexander Cozens. *The Cloud*, (8½ by 12½ in, 21·6 by 31·8 cm; D. L. T. and A. P. Oppé Collection)

associations that the painting aroused in the mind of the spectator. Such a view tends to distinguish, to separate out, the purely visual qualities of a painting irrespective of its subject-matter, and from it the ultimate development to a purely abstract art of design and colour is logical. In some of Cozens's work too the romantic symbols of the infinite, sky and sea, and dizzy contrast of deepest shadow against dazzling light [47], are already stressed, and even in his more conventional ideal landscapes, unpeopled, there are echoes of lonely immensity.

One of the most remarkable of English draughtsmen however was still working in an essentially older technique. Thomas Rowlandson is in fact more draughtsman than watercolourist; his use of wash colour is strictly to enhance his cavorting line, and the only quality, for which he might be suspected of romantic leanings, is his unwearying devotion to sheer excess. Most of his innumerable drawings are of course on the borderline of caricature, if not actually over it, and

48. Thomas Rowlandson. *The Drunken Husband*, (6¼ by 8 in,
15·9 by 20·3 cm; British Museum, London)

he must stand here as representative of the brilliant school of English
caricaturists of his time. One of these, James Gillray, primarily a
political cartoonist and of the first rank as such, was also a true
romantic expressionist in that the follies and vices of his creatures
are not merely displayed but warp and contort their shapes till
they seem to personify themselves. Unlike Gillray, or Hogarth,
Rowlandson was rarely satirical in a didactic or a political way; he
was content simply to upset the apple-cart, and did so with exuberant
talent. For him the decorum of Reynolds existed to be turned upside
down, so displaying usually enormous thighs and harvest-moon
buttocks in a skirl of skirts; he is no artist for the faint-hearted. Here
there is no cry of protest at the folly or the absurdity of the human
breed, but simply a delighted record of that folly and absurdity in
their most extravagant shape, their vitality matched only by the
vitality, curvetting like a bouncing rubber ball, of his draughtsman-
ship [48]. Much of the same exuberance appears in his rarer land-

scape drawings; these are rural picturesque scenes, close in mood and characterization to the farmscapes in oils of his friend Morland: a plump land full of plump rustics and plump animals, but seen with a brisk freshness of vision and the irresistible rhythm of contour that runs through all his work, although his summary treatment of detail (see especially his formula for trees) is confined to the old convention.

The full transition of the eighteenth-century watercolour into the nineteenth-century manner is epitomized in the development of the brilliant, brief-lived Thomas Girtin, who died in 1802 in his twenty-eighth year. His early work dealt with strictly accurate topography, drawings of architectural subjects made for an antiquary. But by 1795 he was working with Turner, his exact contemporary, copying from Cozens and other masters in the house of the collector and patron, Dr Monro, who seems to have run what almost amounted to an academy for young artists. With astonishing speed the young artist matured, and his range widened; he travelled extensively, and in the last five years of his life he achieved for the English watercolour a new independence, in which directness of observation was matched and inspired by a magnificent pictorial imagination that discarded worn-out conventions of composition.

Girtin's view of the *Rue St-Denis* reproduced here [49] is a very late work, and relates to a series of views of Paris that he made in 1801. This is very far from being an exact architectural description; rather, it becomes a sort of triumphant architectural blues, in procession up the street to the great climax of the arch. The windows and doorways, the flagpoles, become not so much details of buildings as an almost musical notation, flickering and dancing along the broad areas of colour. Another version of this composition shows the street crowded with figures; here, emptied of human beings, it becomes its own sufficient drama, the street deep and sheer as a canyon, yet advancing inexorably up its perspective to vanishing point (the drawing is said to have served as design for a backcloth at one of the London theatres). Girtin and Turner, born in the same year, were in their beginnings almost twin geniuses, although the more restless ambition of Turner was evident even then. Though Turner's remark – 'If Girtin had lived, I should have starved' – is probably apocryphal, it indicates justly the stature of his rival's brief-lived talent, narrower perhaps than Turner's, but less wayward, with a most pure and direct impact.

With Turner and Girtin, as leading landscape draughtsmen about 1800, was ranked John Sell Cotman, the Norfolk painter; though towards the end of his career he lost favour, his are now among the most popular and beloved watercolours. If sometimes he carried Girtin's delight in contrasts of sharply silhouetted masses of colour to a rather over-schematized degree, he had always a remarkably sure feeling for composition, for a superbly decorative design, and his technique was of a wonderfully crisp brilliance and facility. In the *Dismasted Brig* [50], painted at a time of crisis about 1823, his technique is seen at its most accomplished, the helplessness of the stricken ship – a theme to which Romantic painters returned again and again – contrasted with, and emphasized by, the firm design that controls the chaos of the storm. It is one of the most haunting of

49. Thomas Girtin. *Rue St-Denis*, *c*.1802 (15½ by 18¾ in, 39·4 by 47·6 cm; Collection of Sir Edmund Bacon)

50. John Sell Cotman. *Dismasted Brig*, *c.*1823 (7¾ by 12 in, 19·7 by 30·5 cm; British Museum, London)

English watercolours; Cotman nevertheless had the chagrin of seeing it sold at auction in 1836 for seventeen shillings.

By the time of Cotman's death, in 1842, the watercolour had for some time been fully established as a work of art in its own right, and with its proper place no longer only in the portfolios and the drawing-books, but in gilt frames on the walls. In 1797, Dr Monro had 90 drawings framed on the walls of his parlour, and 120 in the drawing-room – of course, Monro was a specialist collector, but this gives an idea of the impending popularity of the art. For the more modest house, for those many patrons who, although they may not have owned staterooms of country-house grandeur, nevertheless owned villas of substance and comfort, the watercolour was the natural form of decoration.

Lawrence and Portraiture

Baudelaire, writing in 1846 about portraiture, distinguished between two kinds. One which can be understood as 'history', such as that practised by David and Ingres; the other described as 'fictional' and 'romantic'. The masters of the latter sort whom he selected were Rembrandt – and Reynolds and Sir Thomas Lawrence. Their method implied the translation of a picture into a poem – 'a poem with all its accessories, a poem full of space and reverie'. It is perhaps unexpected to find Reynolds classified as a great 'romantic' painter, yet, whatever his precepts, his effects, particularly in some of his latest portraits, are romantic: for example, in his portrait of the aged but titanic soldier, Lord Heathfield [42] the whole picture becomes what Coleridge might have called an 'organic' extension of the sitter's character and achievement, a victorious serenity shining through the murk of war; this is more an expression of feeling than a descriptive portrait.

Most of the portraitists who worked in the fifty years after Reynolds's death in 1792 were content to perform within the vastly enlarged scope that he had given to the art; none however matched his stature, and few produced variations of any great novelty or significance upon his themes. Raeburn was one who did; obsessed by light, he was capable of almost hallucinatory vision (such as in the study now at Edinburgh, for the portrait of his son on a pony), in which his sitters seem almost to float, translucent and aerial, in reflected light and shadow [51]. But more generally he favoured this light fiercely focused to emphasize the character of his sitters in their faces. His clientele was mostly Scottish, and almost all his life he worked in Edinburgh, recording with a broad, crisp and lively naturalism the forthright countenances of its burghers. Raeburn was perhaps at his best when confronted by the faces of the very old;

51. Sir Henry Raeburn. *Henry Raeburn on a Grey Pony*, c.1796 (13½ by 9 in, 34·3 by 22·9 cm; National Gallery of Scotland, Edinburgh)

then his account of the experience scored by time upon the human face is often both searching and brilliant.

The true successor to Reynolds was Thomas Lawrence, and Reynolds recognized him as such when the young prodigy was barely twenty. *Elizabeth Farren* [52], exhibited in the Academy of 1790, was painted probably in Lawrence's twenty-first year; owing much to Reynolds, it has also a sort of nervous sensitivity and a sensuous dexterity of paint that are quite foreign to the older master. Sheer elegance and poise herald the revival of court portraiture that Lawrence was to accomplish – a vision of aristocracy that in mood goes back to Van Dyck rather than Reynolds. Like Van Dyck, Lawrence was a courtier-painter, and it was the most eminent figures of his time who were to precipitate his finest masterpieces, the set of portraits of the victorious Allied statesmen that he painted after Waterloo and which now adorn the Waterloo Chamber at Windsor Castle. The portrait of Pope Pius VII [53] is perhaps the finest of all. 'I have painted him full in front, with all but the eyes direct to you, with every detail of his countenance (and it is one of many minute parts, but these animated with benevolence, and a sort of mild energy, that is the real character of his intellect and nature).' Strength and sweetness merge in this portrait in the best kind of idealization; it has almost a scent, like a ripe apple in a closed room. But he was also a consummate painter, not so much of women *per se*, as of the romance of woman. The *Elizabeth Farren* is a stunning document of romance, and its sitter almost an epitome of Lawrence's talent; she was an actress who married into the aristocracy (she became the Countess of Derby). Throughout his work, Lawrence tended to depict the aristocracy in the light of an essentially stage glamour. He himself was a keen amateur actor, and intimate friend of the Siddonses and the Kembles; perhaps because he was so deeply in sympathy with the theatre, his portraits, theatrical though they are, at their best (Lawrence like all English portraitists painted too much and his work is very uneven) come across with fresh and living conviction; if his sitters seem to be putting on a show, they do it with conviction, body and soul, and project across the footlights a heightened version of themselves. Miss Farren is perhaps acting a little the part of a lady of high degree (what is she doing in *those* clothes, dewy as gossamer though they be, out in the fields?), but no one will deny

52. Sir Thomas Lawrence. *Elizabeth Farren, later Countess of Derby*, 1790
(94 by 57½ in, 238·8 by 146·1 cm; Metropolitan Museum of Art,
New York)

53. Sir Thomas Lawrence. *Pope Pius VII*, 1819 (104 by 57 in, 264·2 by 144·8 cm; Windsor Castle)

that she carries it off. The painter Northcote (a rival, and doubtless jealous) once described Lawrence as a 'man-milliner sort of painter, a meteor of fashion'; in part the criticism is just, but it also underlines Lawrence's real achievements and relevance; for him, clothes, in the fluent brilliant sheen of his paint, become a necessary extension of his sitter, as though plumage of birds of paradise. He revealed romanticism in the drawing-room; it must be remembered – and Lawrence does not fail to remind you – that he was the visual stage-manager of Regency society, one of the most sophisticated periods ever known, and the prophets of that society were on the one hand the slightly demonic mysterious figure of Byron, and on the other, the austere and perfect silhouette of the arch-Dandy, Brummell, for whom the problem of one's physical presentation in society was almost one of metaphysics.

Constable

Lawrence's achievement is perhaps now underrated (is this from a puritan distrust of a supreme cunning of the hand?), and the three Romantic geniuses usually placed head and shoulders above their contemporaries are Constable, Turner, and Blake. They are so essentially different one from the other that it is difficult to compare their stature. Such comparisons are in any case idle except when they shed light on the figures concerned; Constable himself once said that 'it is difficult to establish superiority in these things', going on to quote a remark of Opie's about Titian, to the effect that Titian, though perhaps not the best painter in the world, produced the best pictures. It is a comment that applies, reversed, almost to Constable himself; if somehow, unaccountably, he did not produce the greatest paintings in English art, he is still the greatest of English painters.

One of the difficulties about Constable is that of seeing his work objectively; once you have come into contact with Constable the man, it is very hard to see his work other than in the sympathetic light of admiration and friendship. He was quite simply an enchanting human being, completely human down to the irascibilities and the dislikes that were stronger than reason warranted; a warm man, content to accept the human condition, and very much of his time, yet compromising on no essential point of his beliefs. Once one has read Keats's letters, the knowledge of them cannot but affect the reading of his poems for ever after; so it is with Constable's letters and his painting. Yet it is important to be as unsentimental about Constable's painting as possible; to see it otherwise is to depreciate it.

In his writings he insisted on science almost as much as upon art:

Painting is a science, and should be pursued as an inquiry into the laws of nature. Why then, may not landscape painting be considered as a branch of natural philosophy, of which pictures are but the experiments?

54. John Constable. *Cloudscape*, (10 by 11½ in, 25·4 by 29·2 cm;
Royal Academy of Arts, London)

That rift which now splits what are known as the Two Cultures –
of science and of the arts – for him did not exist. Science was the
method of art; the purpose of art was poetry. He noted with approval
a remark of his friend Jackson, that the whole object and difficulty of
art is 'to unite nature with imagination'. His scrutiny of the facts of
nature was pertinacious, and as ruthless as it could be in context of
the then state of knowledge; what he abhorred above all was the
second-hand in art, especially academic mannerism. He was even
against the founding of the National Gallery, because he thought
that, with such a collection easily available, 'the manufacturers of
pictures [would] then be made the criterion of perfection, and not
nature'. The function of the artist should be not to imitate art: all
that his predecessors could offer him was experience, in the light of

which he could 'get at nature more surely'. Thus he interested himself in the study of colour, its theory and its chemistry; he became almost a professional meteorologist, and after the appearance of Luke Howard's classification of cloud-formations about 1818/20, he became a tireless sketcher of pure cloudscape – 'skying', he called it [54]. His finished exhibition pictures most often depend on a whole

55. John Constable. *Brighton Beach with Colliers*, 1824 (5¾ by 9¾ in,

series of studies of detail; the case-history, noted as scrupulously as any scientific data, on the back of his sketch of *Brighton Beach with Colliers* [55], is typical of his method: '3rd tide receding left the beach wet – Head of Chain Pier Beach Brighton July 19, Evg., 1824.'

In spite of his insistence on working direct from the source, his

14·6 by 24·8 cm; Victoria and Albert Museum, London)

56. John Constable. *View at Epsom, c.* 1808 (11 by 13¼ in, 27·9 by 33·3 cm; Tate Gallery, London)

purpose was never – as the most superficial glance at his work makes abundantly clear – to produce a purely scientific description, a catalogue of category and detail. Art literally imitating nature was for him, besides being impossible, as pointless as art imitating art. When the Diorama, a vast painted panoramic contraption of landscape (it had something in common with the modern Cinerama) was imported for show from France in 1823, Constable found it without the pale of art, 'because its object is deception'. All that Constable aimed to do, scientifically, was to project the most faithful account possible of the *impression* that the scene before him made on his eye. But he knew that the eye is not a machine, to register like a camera; to attempt such a mechanical account would be (as he once accused a colleague of doing) painting nature without the heart in it. The human painter has to select, and he selects according to what excites him most. We know what excited Constable most – a drama, a play and contrast of colour in a lighter key than had been attempted before: a brilliance, a freshness that registers on skin and palate almost as much as on the eyes, and that can be seen even in such an early sketch as the *View at Epsom* [56] of about 1808; such greens, such yellows, would and did startle his contemporaries ('Take away that nasty green thing!' said a fellow-painter once, in Constable's presence, not realizing that the painting was by him). But the organ that is most excitable in the human make-up is not the eye, but what is loosely known as the heart, and it was with heart and eye that Constable responded. The impression of the eye, in transit to the painter's hand, is affected by the whole nervous and imaginative condition, the state of sensibility, of its owner at the moment he sees. I did not quote the whole of Constable's note on the back of his *Brighton Beach with Colliers;* it goes on: 'My dear Maria's [his wife's] birthday. Your Goddaughter – very lovely Evening – looking Eastward – Cliffs & light of a dark grey effect – background – very white and golden light.' The little painting becomes an exclamation

57. John Constable. *Dedham Mill*, 1820 (21¼ by 30 in, 54 by 76·2 cm; Victoria and Albert Museum, London)

58. John Constable. *View on Hampstead Heath*, *c.* 1823 (13 by 19½ in, 33 by 49·6 cm, Tate Gallery, London)

of love, a birthday salute, as light and fresh and aerial in the eye as a lyric by Wordsworth in the ear. The sea's edge curves, taut as a bow from the blue, and the wind comes with it through the immense sky. 'Lovely' – he noted on another occasion – 'so much so that I could not paint for looking.'

One of the most famous passages in his letters can serve to complement a more wrought-out painting, the *Dedham Mill* [57] of 1820:

The sound of water escaping from mill-dams etc., willows, old rotten planks, slimy posts, and brickwork – I love such things. Shakespeare could make everything poetical; he tells of poor Tom's haunts among 'sheep-cotes and mills'. These have always been my delight. . . . Painting is with me but another word for feeling, and I associate my 'careless boyhood' with all that lies on the banks of the Stour. These scenes made me a painter, and I am grateful – that is, I had often thought of pictures of them before I ever touched a pencil. . . .

Many things lie under the surface of this statement; for one, his abandonment of the 'grand manner'; no classical references, gods or goddesses, inhabit his paintings. Yet his purpose was moral, even as he thought that of painters like Claude had been; he too would have his pictures full (as he felt Gaspar Poussin's were) 'of religious and moral feeling', showing 'how much of his own nature God has implanted in the mind of man'. In this near-religious attitude to landscape of the 'lowest' order he was of course in sympathy with the greatest poets of his age, especially Wordsworth, who answered from such 'a passion and an appetite' to the meanest things in the countryside. And as with Wordsworth, it is Constable's 'lyrics', the swift sketches, that come through with the sharpest urgency and beauty to our eyes today. In his more elaborate, built-up, 'finished' paintings, it often seems as though something had been lost in the process (which was always for Constable very arduous), a vitality for which the greater weight and complexity does not entirely compensate. Yet the 'finished' pictures are what he would wish to be judged by; they are the restatement in modern terms of the grand manner of the past; the sketches were preparatory – 'a sketch . . . will not serve more than one state of mind, and will not serve to drink at again and again'. If one accepts that most of his finished pictures do not quite live up to the implications of the sketches then one may feel that though perhaps the greatest painter in England, he did not paint the greatest pictures. On the other hand, he has surely had a more profound influence on the way we see the landscape of England than anyone else; how much more true to Constable himself are the words he once applied to Wilson – 'one of the great appointments to show the world the hidden stores and beauties of nature; one of the great men who show to the world what exists in nature but which was not known before his time'. One who enlarged the capacity of our experience.

Another point that emerges from his *credo* quoted above, is, for all his new vision, his admitted and modest dependence on, and admiration for, the great painters of the past. 'These scenes . . . I had often thought of pictures of them before I ever touched a pencil.' He saw them in fact, framed in the mind's eye, in a tradition that reaches back through his beloved Gainsborough to his equally beloved Ruysdael, of a painting by whom he wrote: 'The whole is so true, clear and fresh, and as brisk as champagne; a shower has not long passed.' Claude and Poussin he likewise adored, but always in

59. John Constable. *A Country Lane*, c. 1826 (8 by 11¾ in, 20·3 by 29·9 cm; Tate Gallery, London)

the sense of fellow-experimenters on whose experience he could draw 'to get at nature more surely' on his own. Thus in the later sketch, *A Country Lane* [59] of about 1826, one can see the hand of a master who has learnt from Gainsborough and from the Dutch, but who is here applying his fully mature technique for his own original purposes. Never before had anyone thus snatched down in paint the sunlight flying through trees and clouds in the moist English air.

Constable's immediate influence in England was not great; it was more forceful in France, in part and momentarily on Delacroix himself, and most lastingly on the Barbizon school. In France indeed was working an English-born painter who is in many ways reminiscent of Constable – Bonington, domiciled in France from the age of sixteen until his premature death at twenty-six in 1828. He was a close friend of Delacroix, and in his figure-studies, though they are all on a small scale, he surpasses Delacroix in the force of his rhythm, which almost rivals Rubens. In his landscapes there is, besides Bonington's unique poetry of hazy distance, that same high key, and

60. Richard Parkes Bonington. *A Scene in Normandy*, *c.* 1820
(13 by 17¼ in, 33 by 43·9 cm; Tate Gallery, London)

the freshness and tang of dew that recalls Constable. In the so-called
A Scene in Normandy [60] (it is more probably located on the plain of
Saint Denis, near Paris), his crisp and brilliant paint is seen at its best,
with that characteristic deft placing of the brightly lit accents that
looks forward to some of the airy paintings of Boudin.

Turner

Joseph Mallord William Turner was Constable's senior by a year, but outlived him by fourteen. Their careers were as contrasted as their characters. Constable started slowly, almost clumsily, as if groping for the true direction of his genius, and only really began to sight success when he was about forty. Turner swept to the top heights of the profession in his early twenties, borne on by a precocious (and lasting) technical brilliance, a boundless ambition in art and an almost incredible capacity for work (he left to the nation close on 300 oil paintings that he had not sold, or had bought back, and some 19,000 watercolours). Constable's character is open and clear as a bell, and he wrote his own testament in his letters almost as vividly as in his pictures. The sources of Turner's character are veiled; indeed, as a person, he beetles through the history of English art almost like an animated cartoon character, squat and a little dirty, furtive sometimes as an animal, with solitary hideouts, yet apparently welcome and rewarding company in houses as grand as Petworth; mean as a stone in money-matters, yet generous in his death (in his – partly frustrated – bequest). Though he fancied himself as poet, he was, verbally, almost incapable of self-expression and communication; but to compensate for that (as well of course as in his painting), he was granted (not that he relished the gift) in his old age a Voice, the resonance of which matches the splendour of his paint: the full eloquence of Ruskin, his passionate apologist and his prophet.

Because of his immense output, and of the variety and the frequently dubious condition in which much of it has survived, it is difficult to be confident that one has arrived at a reliably comprehensive view of his achievement – and Turner was very conscious of his work as a whole – 'What is the good of them but all together?' But

61. J. M. W. Turner. *The Shipwreck*, 1805 (67½ by 95 in,
171·5 by 241·3 cm; Tate Gallery, London)

it seems clear that his career was basically a constant investigation
into light, and a lifelong love affair with paint: the painting of light
was his business. Constable too was profoundly concerned with
light, and the two in certain oil-sketches can come very close, but for
Turner light was the divine principle of the world, the hero-god of
his pictures; and it has such a Shiva-like function, the creator and
destroyer. The material world only exists in the eye when created by
light; it was Turner's theme to show how light also dissolved all
matter into its own qualities, the colours of the prism. His pictures
are as heroic as any paintings in the classic grand manner, but they
are truly superhuman; man and his works are equally subject with
the landscape to dissolution by light. Light is triumphant, and one
may suspect that for Turner it was almost – if one may put it so – a
personification of power. In his most tremendous pictures, it gener-
ates and unleashes elemental storm and disaster; it fires the wind
that heaves the sea into murder, and the drowning human beings are

62. J. M. W. Turner. *Grand Canal, Venice,* 1835 (36 by 48⅛ in, 91·4 by 122·2 cm; Metropolitan Museum of Art, New York)

swept anonymous as shoals of shrimps to death. You do not hear their screams, only the roar of the storm. Even in his visions of calm, inspired so often by Claude whom he admired so much, the sun, dissolving phoenix-wise in its own pyre, dissolves the solid world with it in its incandescence.

The earliest of his paintings reproduced here is one of many evocations of the sea that obsessed him: *The Shipwreck* [61] of 1805. It was painted at a time when he was still bent on showing his powers in direct rivalry with the masters of the past, and this is an essay on a theme first stated in England by the Van de Veldes, but in terms infinitely more naturalistic, and more violent. The drama of light is not yet the dominant one; as composition it is anchored firmly in the two repeating bright triangles of the sails (although the tilt of these, as if in counterpoint, speaks literally of disaster); through them a strong diagonal thrust comes up and out from the livid light on the horizon on the left, the swirling undulation of the

63. J. M. W. Turner. *Burning of the Houses of Parliament*, 1834 (36 by 47 in, 91·4 by 119·4 cm; Philadelphia Museum of Art)

trough of the huge white wave that will break in the next second over the wallowing rowing-boat. In the next picture in time [62] – it is of thirty years later, 1835 – light proceeds calmly about its business, but transmuting none the less firmly all things into its own terms, until they become dreams or ghosts of substance, holding but tenuously to their physical dimensions and identities under the insidious assault of reflection and refraction; the weight of the black gondola seems less than that of its shadow. The Venice that Canaletto once painted sharp as diamonds is drowning, awash with light. About the same time, Turner also showed one of his several recordings of the *Burning of the Houses of Parliament* [63]. (This happened on the night of 16 October 1834, and Turner, judging by the visual memoranda in a notebook in the British Museum, went out to watch and record.) The scene becomes an almost apocalyptic vision, with the dark huddled mass of spectators swagged hushed across the foreground, powerless and hypnotized. What is left of the world is no more than a reflection of fire; the twin towers of Westminster Abbey (on whose ghostly uprights the composition holds together) seem to float in the flames, and the far end of the bridge to disintegrate into them. The painting made a great impression when first shown; although it mystified people, the impact was so undeniable that it was accepted. A critic wrote in the *Spectator:*

> The execution of the picture is curious; to look at it close, it appears a confused mass of daubs and streaks of colour; yet we are told the painter worked at it within a few inches of the canvas for hours together without stepping back to see the effect. Turner seems to paint slovenly – daubing as one would say; yet what other painter preserves equal clearness of colour? Not that we like this scene-painting manner; we should prefer being able to look at a picture near as well as at a distance; but such a one as this we are content to look at in any way the artist chooses – with all its faults.

It is a remarkable example of Turner's capacity for holding the relation of the parts of an immensely complicated subject clear in his mind right through its long execution to the end: a capacity for coordination which is of genius. When it was shown at the British Institution, it arrived, according to a fellow-contributor, in a state 'like chaos before creation'. For three hours before the show opened, Turner worked on it, and when he had done, it stood stable and ordered as architecture; in that final modulation, done mostly with the palette knife, he did no more than 'tune' the colour and place the accents, and the picture cohered. When he had finished, 'with his face still turned to the wall, and at the same distance to it, [he] went sidling off, without speaking a word to anyone. . . . All looked with a wondering smile, and Maclise remarked, "There, that's masterly; he does not stop to look at his work; he *knows* it is done, and he is off."'

But a picture shown seven years later, the *Snow Storm* [64] of 1842, which now seems one of his most prophetic and original paintings, was not so warmly greeted. Here he had gone a bit too far ahead of his time for his generation to be able to accept his experiment, let alone understand and be fired by it. It is sometimes said to be unfinished, but Turner alone was ever competent to decide that point. He himself was uncertain about it; his account of its genesis is almost incredible when you realize that Turner was sixty-seven when it happened. The full title was *Snow Storm – Steam-boat*

64. J. M. W. Turner. *Snow Storm*, 1842 (36 by 48 in, 91·4 by 121·9 cm; National Gallery, London)

off a harbour's mouth making signals in shallow water and going by the lead, and Turner himself was out there, on the Admiralty steam packet *Ariel*, off Harwich in a great storm in January 1842:

I got the sailors to lash me to the mast to observe it; I was lashed for four hours and I did not expect to escape, but I felt bound to record it if I did. But no one had any business to like it.

The critics agreed, but Turner was annoyed by the scale of their scorn; it was called 'a fantastic puzzle' and generally lampooned; its comparison with a 'mass of soapsuds and whitewash' particularly vexed its author:

I wonder what they think the sea's like? I wish they'd been in it.

'Pictures of nothing and very like it', said a contemporary. The *Snow Storm*, though even to modern eyes not immediately obvious

117

65. J. M. W. Turner. *Bellinzona from the South*, 1841 (9 by 13 in, 22·9 by 33 cm; British Museum, London)

to read, is not about nothing, and it is very highly organized. It might perhaps be called an attempt to paint nowhere – the loss of all points of reference in a blizzard at sea when the only constant left is the swirling slash of snow and water and smoke. It is also an attempt to convey the material power, the blind, shoving weight, of the flurries of snow, spray and wave; further, it is a curiously personal statement of triumph, of sheer survival. The dynamic centre that spins the picture is the dark wheel of the paddleboat, which seems to churn the world outward from itself into centrifugal paroxysm, and it is not, here, the elements that converge destructively on the human ship.

The vision called *Bellinzona from the South* [65] is a page from one of Turner's sketch books, probably relating to his Swiss visit of 1841, and is moving closer to the abstract than the *Snow Storm;* it is very far from the accurate, topographical kind of drawing on which Turner had served his apprenticeship. The 'story' is about a vision of colour, luminous drifts of colour; across and through these, the light outlines that spell towers, castles, and rock run frail as lace, insubstantial. In such drawings, the colour dropped like shining veils across the white background, the degree of dependence of Turner's oil technique on such watercolour exercises is indicated. There are thousands of them and in the latter stages they become often purely abstract memoranda of the patterns of depth that contrasting and complementing patches of colour create on the flat white paper. His pursuit of colour was largely empirical, but based also on a study of theory. His annotated copy of the English translation

66. J. M. W. Turner. *Peace: Burial of Wilkie at Sea*, 1841–2 (32½ by 32½ in, 88·6 by 88·6 cm; Tate Gallery, London)

67. J. M. W. Turner. *Chichester Channel*, 1829 (25 by 53½ in,

(1840) of Goethe's *Farbenlehre*, for example, still exists, and he even titled a picture at the Academy in 1843 *Light and Colour* (*Goethe's Theory*); Goethe, among other things, associated particular colours with particular states of mind, a counterpoint that can be followed in some of Turner's compositions.

Turner's reflection of the sympathies of his time scarcely needs stressing; he was the most complete expounder in visual terms of the literary and emotional themes of Romanticism – the romance of

63·5 by 135·9 cm; Tate Gallery, London)

Walter Scott, the cult of nature, particularly in its extreme gestures of soaring mountain, of shoreless sea (the archetypal romantic image perhaps) and incandescent sky [66,67]; his castles are battlemented, haunted, and often in ruins. But also, in so many ways, he points forward out of his time. In his investigation of colour he anticipates in some degree the practice of the Impressionists; in some late works, when colour seems to become arbitrary in the sense that it is independent of the forms it no longer describes, he anticipates sometimes the Fauves, and more often certain of the twentieth-century Expressionists and the purely abstract painters – and still, in the fifties and sixties of this century, his relevance is acute. Already in 1799, he told Farington that he had no 'settled process', but 'drove the colours about till he had expressed the Idea in his mind' – a statement which, isolated, and given only the slightest of twists, could have been made by an Action painter. In fact, in certain of his later pictures all attempt at shaping the composition in any way hitherto understood has vanished, and it depends on the tensions and gestures of the paint's run, slash, and flood of colour alone.

Blake

Earlier, I quoted William Blake on the gospel of 'particularizing', and the heresy of 'generalizing'. Yet, it is obvious that he generalized in his visual work to a degree that his contemporaries had no hesitation in qualifying as 'like mad'. But if we look into Blake's vocation more closely, the meaning of what he called 'particularizing' becomes clearer. A firm anti-governmental radicalism influenced all that he did; not least among his hatreds was 'official' art; this certainly sharpened his odium of Reynolds, President of the Academy, and of naturalistic landscape. His whole life was spent in relative poverty and obscurity, and he was never the centre of any sort of fashionable enclave. Looking back, he wrote that 'Inspiration and Vision' was from his youth 'and now is, and I hope will always remain, my element, my eternal dwelling place'. He was the personal visionary, the individualist; the only external authority that he was prepared to admit was that of his own inspiration. To particularize, for Blake, meant simply to do what your private, particular, vision told you to do; he looked within rather than without, and depicted this inner vision. The human make-up being what it is, however, the vision could not but embody itself in a shape strongly influenced by what his eye had absorbed, and that from other art rather than from nature. He drew on Michelangelo (as did Reynolds and Lawrence), and also on ancient Greek sculpture and English Gothic forms. In his exhibition catalogue of 1809, he promised 'real art, as it was left us by Raphael and Albert Dürer, and Julio Romano, stripped from the ignorances of Rubens and Rembrandt, Titian and Correggio, by William Blake'. But, abandoning scientific perspective, and any attempt at naturalistic illusion, he used his eclectic anatomy of art in a way that was at once decorative, symbolic, and essentially spiritual. To understand the origins of his art, it must be remembered that he was trained as an engraver, was one of the greatest lyric poets ever to use the English language, and was also the profuse prophet of a new and still imperfectly understood mythology. His painting is normally watercolour (or a variation of it – he was a vigorous technical experimenter), and, rather than water-colour, more strictly coloured drawing; it has always something of the book illustration about it, and his experiments in book production were remarkable and original, an attempt to fuse image and word, as in the colour-printed and hand-tinted *Prophetic Books*. The essential surge and exhilaration of his drawing comes from what he called the 'flaming line', and his art – which escapes from European canons of what is art as does late Elizabethan painting (both are very difficult to export to foreign taste) – is the supreme example of what is generally held (though how Reynolds or Turner are accommodated to this opinion is hard to see) to be a specific, essential quality of the English visual character – the emphasis on line. Yet perhaps his paintings are better described as poems visualized than as illustrations: dream a dream and lasso it with a line. If their literal interpretation is often obscure (when dependent on his own obscure religious mythology), their intense vitality and exhilaration, and their spiritual grandeur, have a naked and direct impact, and do not fail his inspiration. The *Adam and Eve and the Archangel Raphael* [68] was in fact designed as an illustration (one of a series for *Paradise Lost* made in 1808) and is entirely lucid. Adam, Eve, echo Michelangelo and Greek sculpture; the 'scene' is framed as in an engraved border, by a schematized foliage as crisp and vital as English 'stiff-leaf' carving from Southwell. Raphael's wings burn ceaselessly in a perfect ogee, which is also the hallucinatory shape of a candle flame. Such is the intensity of this hybrid, and its perfect coordination, that it lives on in its own life, although if described in terms of normal iconography and style analysis, it could only sound slightly absurd. Mysterious, luminous, and haunting as an illuminated initial from a medieval manuscript, it is as crisp with enduring vitality as the not dissimilar forms of Fuseli, Blake's contemporary to whom he owed so much, are now flaccid. (To dismiss Fuseli so briefly is unjust; yet it is only in his drawings that his great intellectual capacity and the fervour of his vision seem to be matched by his practice.)

68. William Blake. *Adam and Eve and the Archangel Raphael*, 1808
(15⅝ by 19½ in, 39·7 by 49·6 cm; Museum of Fine Arts, Boston)

69. William Blake. *Pity*, c. 1795 (16⅝ by 21⅛ in, 42·2 by 53·7 cm; Tate Gallery, London)

Blake's attitude to art was symptomatic; once all authority is cast off, and the standards that remain appear to be entirely intuitive and subjective, it becomes much harder for the average spectator to understand his work. For the genius, as Blake was, this does not in the end matter, as the mysterious vitality that genius inspires into its works endures, and will continue to get its response. But for the average artist who relies upon inspiration but does not possess it, this attitude means that his work will be still-born, not even enjoyable as an exercise in a tradition. At all levels except the highest, communication between artist and spectator will tend to break down. Blake's contemporaries, quite naturally, said that Blake was mad, even as Picasso is still held today to be mad by certain circles. Blake was not mad; he was an explorer, a crotchety English eccentric, and a genius; he had visions and set them out for all to see. On 12 August 1827, he 'sang loudly and with true ecstatic energy and seemed so happy that he had finished his course', and at six that evening he died. His song continues, and so do his pictures, even if they rarely capture so fully the complete, sharp purity of the lyrics.

The spiritual, almost revivalist fervour of Blake for art found its disciples towards the close of his life among a band of enthusiastic, very young men who had come to know him, and their careers illustrate something of the glories and perils of the visionary's way of art. The peril is – as Blake himself never quite did – to lose the vision.

70. William Blake. *Tree with Crescent Moon*, 1812 woodcut for Virgil's *Pastorals* ($1\frac{5}{16}$ by $2\frac{7}{8}$ in, 3·4 by 7·3 cm; British Museum, London)

This group, notably George Richmond, John Linnell (rather older than the others), and especially Samuel Palmer, were responsible for a brief flowering of pastoral art, and are associated with the name of the village of Shoreham in Kent. It lasted less than ten years and then they went their ways: Richmond to become a polished rather hygienic taker of portrait-likenesses ('The truth? Yes, but the truth lovingly told'); Linnell to become a prosperous, though slightly eccentric and lush painter of rustic sweeps of Surrey; Palmer to become an able Victorian watercolourist in the mainstream tradition. Yet Palmer's early drawings and watercolours stand alone in English art; though he was certainly influenced by Blake's woodcuts for the *Pastorals* of Virgil – 'visions of little dells, and nooks, and corners of Paradise; models of the exquisitest pitch of intense poetry' [70] – his description of them fits many of his own pictures more aptly than Blake's; from the latter he inherited rather a quality of enthusiasm than anything else. He was in line with the then widespreading passion of Christian nature mysticism, and moved

71. Samuel Palmer. *Young Man Yoking an Ox*, *c.* 1831 (5 by 7¼ in, 15 by 18·4 cm; Ashmolean Museum, Oxford)

especially by the pastoral poems of Milton. His paintings are often drawn out of the night or the dusk, heavy with silence and the slow swell of ripening; they are perhaps the densest pictures in English art, their design as closewoven, as organic, as the cell-structure of a living organism. The sun sets on them only for a huge moon to reveal with shadow what the sun hid, a more primeval, essential shape for the world. They are also the most truly blessed pictures painted in England since the Renaissance, landscapes of contemplation and adoration.

The peace, this sense of unity and of serenity, abides in the *Young Man Yoking an Ox* of about 1831 [71]. Six or seven years later, the intensity failed, the vision faded, and Palmer became an 'ordinary' painter. The organic coherence of his work had gone for ever; there is often even some confusion of organization as the eye travels from foreground to background (one need only glance for comparison at Turner's *Bellinzona from the South* to see where Palmer's later views fall to prose). There are dozens of Victorian watercolourists of this kind, and of this agreeable, able, but uninspiring level.

Early Victorian Painting

Writing about forty years ago, Roger Fry could annihilate, apparently with almost complete justification, almost the whole of English nineteenth-century painting with the exception of the artists of the early part of the period whom I have already discussed – 'the terrible descent in Victorianism' from the heights of achievement of Constable, Turner, even of Wilkie. We have now a longer perspective over the whole period, and, while Fry's contention that it can show no peaks to match those of the preceding age is still clearly uncontestable, we can see that it does possess some very respectable eminences, and that the upper level of the general plateau is by no means so drear as it once seemed.

By the eighteen-thirties, the Royal Academy had achieved much of its purpose for the arts, at least in a social sense; art had become entirely respectable, and so had the artist. The section of the public (enlarging at tremendous rate in the booming prosperity of industrial and imperial England) that was well enough to do to be able to buy paintings did buy them, and did love them in their fashion; the aristocratic patrons of former days began to be matched and even on occasions surpassed by the new millionaires emerging among the commercial middle-classes, men like Vernon, who had made a corner in horse-coping for the army in the Napoleonic wars, or Sheepshanks, from a Yorkshire industrialist family. They might well be more at ease with subjects drawn from everyday life than with the mythological and often obscure anecdotes of which the Old Masters were so fond. Art became a flourishing concern, with a solid and efficient organization, the Academy its stock exchange. The trouble often lay in what this concern was concerned about, and above all in the manner of its concern. The ends – truths through pictorial experiment – tend to be lost from sight in the profusion of the means. There is the attempt not so much to lay bare and to analyse a fresh emotion, as to copy a conventional expression of an emotion. Take for example painting in the grand manner; that remarkable diarist but generally indifferent painter Benjamin Robert Haydon, might seem to have sealed the fate of the vain quest of British painters to create masterpieces of historical painting when, after a bitter life driven to despair by that very quest, he ended it by his own hand in June 1846, leaving his vast canvas of *Alfred and the First British Jury* unfinished and splashed with his blood. Yet such painting was apparently still outwardly flourishing, artificially nourished by commissions such as those for the decoration of the new Houses of Parliament, where you can still see the antique gestures deployed; but they are the gestures of an obsolete rhetoric lacking all urgency. The truly monumental expressions of the early Victorian spirit were made in other spheres, and inspired by realities of new achievement and discovery; such were the Crystal Palace, the great railway stations. In more modest kinds of painting, there is a tendency to take an immediately recognizable likeness of a subject already known to be a reliable stimulus to a certain emotion in its beholder; thus a careful painting of a picturesque grouping of trees and water, or of characters in period costume, or of rustics in a farmyard, may arouse the same response in the spectator as the sight of the actual objects themselves. But that, as Constable said indignantly, is not the end of art; it is deception. Yet on the other hand, it is undeniably an ingredient in the pleasures offered by the vast majority of all European post-Renaissance pictures, and the pleasures often allied with it – of colour, of skill in craftsmanship, and so on – are none the less real for being of a less exalted order than that sense of revelation, of kindling excitement followed by serene confidence of mind, that a truly great painting can bring. Roger Fry's strictures tend to imply that it is a sin to indulge in contemplation of pictures of a lesser order; it would seem to many rather pretentious, pompous, priggish, and petulant not to indulge in them as long as they retain their savour and one accepts them for what they are.

It may be best, in attempting to indicate some way through the immense profusion of Victorian painting, to select some of the subjects that most obsessed painters and public alike. Portraiture – in spite of the establishment of photography in the forties, which really

72. William Etty. *Venus and Cupid*, c. 1840–5 (27 by 20 in,
68·6 by 50·8 cm; Tate Gallery, London)

knocked all the urgency out of this branch of art, previously the *only*
way in which a man could preserve his physical vanity from oblivion
– continued perennial. Sir David Wilkie, who in his earlier manner
had painted some brilliant small-scale portraits, later attempted the
grand romantic scale with formidable flamboyance incorporating

sometimes, a startlingly intransigent and dour searching of his sitter's features; but he died perhaps before he had realized the full potential of his latent originality. William Etty too painted some striking portraits of ripeness, but is best known of course as the only English specialist in the nude [72] – nudes that seem nowadays of entire sexual propriety, though they alarmed Victorian opinion and are often of a lush and admirable proficiency. But generally the romantic overtones and the brilliance of Lawrence's manner gradually evaporated as the Victorian presentation portrait came into its own – formal effigies, state-portraits, often curiously close in aloofness of temper to Elizabethan portraits – to adorn board-rooms, town-halls, and public institutions. The outstanding 'public' portrait-painter was certainly George Frederic Watts, who, in his later portraits from 1860 on, sought with tireless persistence to unveil a monument of moral grandeur within his sitters' features – and at times almost succeeded; his characterization of Gladstone [73] conveys something not only of the rock-like endurance of the man, but, what is much rarer in Victorian portraiture, a sense of the nervous passion that illuminated it. There is often a toughness in Watts's male portraits that one would not suspect from his big allegorical (and immensely popular) paintings; Watts loved to paint nudes in a Venetian glow, yet his vision of the flesh is so innocuous that the modern onlooker is baffled to know what the excitement was about. But the most vivid and vital of Victorian portraits were those painted generally by painters who did not specialize in society portraiture; portraits not intended for exhibition, often private portraits of relatives or of friends, and often too, as so much of the best painting of the time, small in scale. The portraits that will stop you to look twice in the galleries are the intense, almost miniature, scrutinies by the Pre-Raphaelites of their friends' faces; even Alma Tadema produced some marvellously solid, plain yet vital, likenesses on a small scale.

In 1862, a grand international exhibition in London was the occasion for an ambitious survey of English painting of the century; an official review of it found that 'the life of our Art in this century lies almost entirely in its Schools of Landscape and Incident: both practically inventions of the last sixty years . . . and a more serious style of Incident has lately become common'. In fact, the glories of the landscape school were already over; its 'Shakespeare', the

73. George Frederic Watts. *Gladstone,* 1858 (25 by 21½ in, 63·5 by 54·6 cm; National Portrait Gallery, London)

writer considered, reasonably, had been Turner, but contemporary academic landscape tended neither to reflect nor develop the experiments of Turner or of Constable, but rather to depend on Dutch models of the seventeenth century. For urban patrons, throughout this period, rural idylls of cows, picturesque trees, and country scenes, retained an inexhaustible attraction. The 'School of Incident' however was a more vital matter, developing out of genre painting, the great success of the century. Its formal sources are mainly in Dutch and Flemish genre painting, a taste for which came into respectability towards the close of the eighteenth century, but in subject-matter it tended also to absorb the themes of history paintings, modulating them to suit the more comfortable and unemphatic requirements of middle-class values; especially, the tragic becomes the pathetic. It is significant that the most popular and acceptable renderings of the ultimate moment were not in human terms at all, but animal ones; in 1853 Ruskin supposed Landseer to be the most popular painter of the day. Mimed out by Scotch terriers, the human predicament became more supportable, while Landseer could also celebrate the last moments of a stag in pictorial language (often of great technical brilliance) of the grand manner.

Pure genre painting got off to a flying start in Britain with the young Wilkie at the very beginning of the century; the Scottish Teniers they called him, master of low-life pictures of village life and festival which, although they sometimes do not fully cohere in composition (the great failing of most English genre, and due partly perhaps to the insistence in the schools of studying the single figure in isolation), they have a charming boisterousness and verve and no element of social satire or overt comment. In the same idiom, Wilkie could also treat a great climactic moment in the national history, and his *Chelsea Pensioners Reading the Gazette of the Battle of Waterloo* [74] struck far more chords in the National breast than did Lawrence's heroic images of the conquerors in the Waterloo Chamber or Haydon's vision of Wellington brooding on the battlefield; it was so popular at the Royal Academy in 1822 that it had to be protected by a special rail to prevent the crowd damaging it in their enthusiasm. He used the same style too for interpretations of scenes from national history, as the history painters were trying to do on a larger scale, but the moment he himself opened up in scale and to a broader, more declamatory style, public favour began to desert him in some measure. The taste not only for small-scale historical pictures but even more for interpretations of medieval romance and scenes from historical fiction grew and flourished throughout the century; Walter Scott's work became the book of countless pictures, costumed and propertied with the same loving (if not always accurate) detail as are the novels themselves. Not only Scott, but all the literary masterpieces of sentiment were raided by the painters for inspiration, especially the *Vicar of Wakefield* and *Gil Blas*. Also some

74. Sir David Wilkie. *Chelsea Pensioners Reading the Gazette of the Battle of Waterloo*, 1822 (36½ by 60½ in, 92·7 by 153·7 cm; Victoria and Albert Museum, Apsley House, London)

75. William Powell Frith. Detail from *Derby Day*, 1856–8 (Tate Gallery, London)

painters began to turn more attention to the contemporary scene, not only the Pre-Raphaelites in the fifties, but others from Mulready to Frith, though it was a long time before, in the seventies, painters like Frank Holl began to produce paintings of a genuine social realism in studies of the lives of the poor (the woodcuts of Holl and Fildes had great influence on Van Gogh's attitude to the function of painting in society). Much of all this, painted in a sound academic technique, still contains considerable charm for most people. Frith's *Derby Day* [75] is at the least brilliant pictorial journalism, even if it conveys perhaps an overall impression of charade rather than of pullulating crowd, a smell of grease-paint rather than of race-course. Such work is after all that of able, intelligent professionals, serious in their work even if seriousness seems often to become confused with moral or technical earnestness. Nor is the flash of a more intense, exploratory creativeness entirely lacking in the Pre-Raphaelites.

The Pre-Raphaelites

The impulse that fired the Pre-Raphaelites was perhaps more purely a moral than an artistic one, but above all theirs was the earnest, ardent – though sadly perishable – sheer enthusiasm of youth. They formed up after the exhibition in 1848 at the Academy of William Holman Hunt's *Flight of Madeline and Porphyro*; Hunt was twenty years old. He, with the young Millais and Rossetti (to whose Italian revolutionary fervour the idea of a secret brotherhood was due) were the most important of them, but Hunt was the only one to persist with the principles of the original credo through a long career. Their main aims were refreshingly straightforward (compare the tortuousness of any artistic manifesto issued nowadays!): to have genuine ideas and to express them, and to study directly from nature. They caused, as young and passionate movements of revolt are wont to do, some scandal which swiftly became a success of scandal and then quite simply success. (It is in fact to their example that the critic of 1862 surely refers: 'the more serious style of Incident lately become common'.) The most striking and original thing about their work is the brilliant colour, though it is in technique a keying up of the method of translucent paint luminous over a pure white ground that had been used years before not only by the Van Eycks but by Wilkie's near contemporary Mulready (whose best work, of landscape or of small boys, generally fighting, has also a rare stability, an as-it-were purely pictorial specific gravity). The English took to this almost garish brilliance without overmuch fuss; foreigners did not – even Taine, here in 1860 and sympathetic to much in English art, wrote: 'Impossible to imagine cruder effects, colour more brutal or exaggerated, more violent and gaudy discords, harder or falser juxtapositions of tones. . . .' Reds, purples, raw greens. 'There can be no doubt,' concluded Taine, 'that there is

something peculiar in the condition of the English retina.' But Taine too was writing conditioned by the conventions of his own time, and to modern eyes re-conditioned by developments in painting from the Fauves to the Hard-Edge school of America, the colour-contrasts flaunted by the Pre-Raphaelites tell more excitingly than ever. Whatever the exact effect of the style of the predecessors of Raphael on the so-called Pre-Raphaelites may have been, they certainly achieved a greater clarity and vividness than any of their contemporaries; they emphasized exact detail with rather angular drawing, while at the same time they managed to convey something of the sharpness, the physical weight, of that detail into the symbolism of their pictures. Millais' *The Blind Girl* is one of the most remarkable even if its symbolism is a little over-stressed; the colour vibrant in the thunder-light, the picture brimming with a stillness that must at any moment crack [76].

The expression of their chief hates in the art of their contemporaries tells one as much and perhaps more than their own programme for achievement. They abhorred 'Monkeyana ideas, Books of Beauty, Chorister Boys, whose forms were those of melted wax with drapery of no tangible texture'; that is, Landseer's humanized animals, slick album depictions of luscious females, and popular soppy paintings of ostentatious piety. And generally the Pre-Raphaelites did manage to avoid the currently besetting sins of the simper, the trite, and the sentimental. On the other hand, their built-in belief in the necessarily elevated and elevating nature of art was entirely of their time, of a well-regulated Puritan code of social behaviour, in which art, the primary appeal of which cannot help but be through the dangerous senses, must be made respectable by a high moral content. If the Pre-Raphaelites were not sentimental, most of their painting was nevertheless well weighted with sentiment. Hunt's famous picture of *The Awakened Conscience* [77] is a textbook case. It shows a loose woman with her lover, in a nest of sin over-furnished with bristling and lavish discomfort. Hunt proceeded personally to such a nest to ensure archaeological documentation of detail (as Toulouse-Lautrec, with markedly different results, was later to do).

76. Sir John Everett Millais. Detail from *The Blind Girl*, 1854–6 (Birmingham City Museum and Art Gallery)

77. William Holman Hunt. *The Awakened Conscience*, 1852–4
(29¾ by 21⅝ in, 75·6 by 64·2 cm; Collection of Sir Colin Anderson)

The woman was shown at the critical moment of redemption, recalled suddenly to memories of innocence by the words of the song, *Oft in the Stilly Night*, open legibly on the piano; she starts from her lover's arms. The expression on her face was later found too ugly – fearful in anguish; Hunt softened it, and changed the title to *The Awakened Conscience*. Here perhaps the tension between

142

78. Arthur Hughes. *April Love*, 1856 (35 by 19½ in, 88·9 by 49·5 cm; Tate Gallery, London)

literature and didacticism and painting is not fused; this, for all its brilliance of detail and its sincerity, like so many works by Hunt's lesser contemporaries, makes comprehensible Taine's lament: 'What a pity it is that these artists, instead of writing, took to painting!' It is slightly reassuring and not entirely irrelevant to note the subsequent history of the model for this picture, the 'siren-like'

Annie Miller. Her conscience remained at least for a time far from awakened, and her conduct exceptionable; Hunt became engaged to her, but proved unable to detach her from 'her old objectionable habits', till he finally broke with her, a breach in which Rossetti played an obscure but apparently dubious part. Years later Hunt met her again on Richmond Hill by chance, 'a buxom matron with a carriage full of children' and bowered in respectability. He then 'forgave' her. Yet, after all that, *The Awakened Conscience*, in its tortured way, is not an image that one easily forgets.

The subject-matter of the painters ranged from the Biblical, the Medieval, Dante (especially of course with Rossetti), Shakespeare, up to contemporary life. They discovered Keats; they illustrated Tennyson. At their best they created images that are more than illustration, but true visual poetry – such as the early visions of Arthur Hughes (not an original member) of young, unrequited, and one suspects mysteriously unrequitable, love, drawn with cool clarity and lilac-fresh in colour [78]; or the sumptuous glowing women of Rossetti, mystic fusions of human and divine love [79]. But the most interesting of them all was perhaps Ford Madox Brown, never a member of the Brotherhood, though a close friend. He applied its principles with a ruthless tenacity in such problem-allegories as his famous *Work*, conceived as a social critique and wrought out in detail that makes the whole hard to read; he could however achieve a rare concentration of vision. *The Pretty Baa-Lambs* [80] is typical of him even in its entire un-prettiness: 'painted almost entirely in sunlight, which twice gave me a fever while painting.' (None of the other Pre-Raphaelites were so determined in their exposure of their persons in the quest for authenticity, though Hunt ran Brown close, and Millais' model for *Ophelia* was immersed dangerously in a bath.) It puzzled people:

I was told it was impossible to make out what *meaning* I had in the picture. At the present moment, few people, I trust, will seek for any meaning beyond the obvious one, that is – a lady, a baby, two lambs, a servant maid, and some grass. In all cases, pictures must be judged first as pictures – a deep philosophical intention will not make a fine picture, such being

79. Dante Gabriel Rossetti. *Mary Magdalene Leaving the House of Feasting*, 1857 (13½ by 7¾ in, 34·3 by 19·7 cm; Tate Gallery, London)

F

rather in excess of the bargain; and though all epic works of art have this excess, yet I should be much inclined to doubt the genuineness of that artist's ideas who never painted from love of the mere look of things, whose mind was always on the stretch for a moral. This picture was painted out in the sunlight; the only intention being to render that effect as well as my powers in a first attempt of that kind would allow.

Its blues are indeed startling, brooding and heavy, but no less startling is the monumental icon-like figure of the mother with the child, and the background is an example of that doting precision which helped to produce, in Brown's *An English Autumn Afternoon*, at Birmingham, one of the truly great English landscapes of the nineteenth century. A tiny picture at the Tate, *Carrying Corn*, is another one, projected on to its canvas by the low sun behind you that lances the long shadows into it; across the broad planes of colour, sharp-edged as on a lantern slide, the detail ripples in the calm of a harvest evening, the pale moon already in the clear sky: a condensation of calm and of achievement.

80. Ford Madox Brown. *The Pretty Baa-Lambs*, 1851–9 (24 by 30 in, 61 by 76·2 cm; Birmingham City Museum and Art Gallery)

High Victorian Painting

The eighteen-fifties was the great decade for the Pre-Raphaelite burst of freshness into English painting; soon after, the fire faded from almost all their work; they were always a collection of fairly opinionated individuals rather than a movement. That quality which at its best has the intensity of a true urgency, and at its worst is shrill (the Pre-Raphaelites were at least very rarely merely comfortable), becomes diffused. Rossetti's visions, from the ripening acidities of his early pictures, blossomed into a lush, hot-house flush of women, sometimes as it were as spiritually over-upholstered as Lely's women are fleshily so. Brown suffered from the influence of Rossetti more than he gained from it; Millais sought a more sonorous poetry in a broader style, and found wealth, success, and a generally coarse though often most virtuoso prose. Hunt, the only one to pursue in militance his original practice, in irascible colour and quirky line, worried most of his later pictures to death. In a slightly younger generation, Burne-Jones, drawing deeply on Rossetti's images and then refining them with reminiscence of the fifteenth-century Italians, dreamed in paint those strange dreams of attenuated figures about their mystic business. 'I mean by a picture,' he said, 'a beautiful romantic dream of something that never was, never will be – in a light better than any light that ever shone – in a land no one can ever define or remember, only desire. . . .' A peculiarly English dream, a visualization of poetry rather than a distillation of the poetry of the visual.

But of course the Pre-Raphaelites were not the only painters, only a rather intenser current in the immense output of paintings through the second half of the century. The fifties also saw the climax of Landseer's reputation and the continuing prosperity of Frith, with his attention too turned to crowd scenes of contemporary life. In

81. J.J.Tissot. *The Gallery of H.M.S. Calcutta, Portsmouth,* 1876
(27 by 36 in, 68·6 by 91·5 cm; Tate Gallery, London)

1855 a distinguished and intelligent Englishman, both painter and
chronicler of art, Richard Redgrave, was in Paris; comparing French
art with English, he found that if English subjects were less 'elevated'
than the French, still they were 'works which a man can live with,
and love to look on, obtruding no terrors on his sleeping or waking
fancies'. At their best, always small, such pictures could sharpen the
dull and modest small-change of social behaviour into gold, as in
the work of Augustus Egg, or later in the seventies in the minutely
detailed paintings of J. J. Tissot [81], in which the poetry of the
ennui of those who have world enough and time is recaptured for
the first time in England since Devis (though Whistler too had something of this quality). It was a boom time, financially, for the
painters; it was a boom time also for the dealers, who now began to
deal and to promote on a large scale the work of living painters.
The main source of profit lay in the copyright of each painting for
reproduction purposes; the improved technique of steel-engraving

now made it possible to publish editions running into thousands, which in the early eighties with the introduction of cheap chromo-lithography became hundreds of thousands. The scale of profit could be fabulous; Gambart paid Hunt £5,775 for the *Finding of Christ in the Temple*, and from it made £4,000 in exhibition fees, £5,000 (profit) from the engraving, and £1,500 from the resale of the painting itself. The vicissitudes of this stock-market in pictures have recently been charted* but the relationship of art itself to this development has yet to be analysed. The temptation to produce pictures with a strong best-selling appeal in terms of engraving must have been very strong, but the qualities that made a best-seller were dubious, particularly the lush and obvious sentiment of subject – Millais' *Cherry Ripe* sold 600,000 impressions as a supplement to the *Graphic* at Christmas 1880. A little later this kind of art found perhaps its proper level, when Millais' *Bubbles* was sold to Pears' Soap, and became in advertisements the widest-known academic picture ever. Many were of course aware of the dangers – Lord Leighton, in his insistence on the necessity of a high 'moral tone' in those who wished to produce great art, diagnosed in the 'sordid appetite', 'the greed for gain', together with the 'vulgar thirst for noisy success', the greatest pitfalls.

Leighton himself is the figurehead of the new movement of High academic Art that rides onwards through the sixties and seventies: benign but aloof, Olympian. Leighton had no wish to see his paint-ings engraved, exposed 'in every cheap print-shop in the country'. Leighton's purposes were of course not anecdotal, but neither were they pietistic nor didactically improving; he was the apostle of high-ideal art, which, by arousing a complex harmony of associations in the spectator (and demanding for this a well-equipped spectator), toned up his whole being, physical, intellectual, moral, and spiritual. In manner he was eclectic (of immense learning) and cosmopolitan, but his was essentially in theory a classic revival, specifically a Hellen-istic one, and equally essentially in practice Victorian. On the bleak uglinesses of the modern urban world outside he closed his windows (glazed perhaps not with glass but with onyx, translucent but not transparent), and within he summoned up, with meticulous tech-nique, those processional compositions of perfect-limbed youths

*G. Reitlinger, *The Economics of Taste*, 1961.

149

82. Albert Moore. *Apples*, 1875 (11½ by 20½ in, 29·2 by 52·1 cm;
W. E. Kenrick Collection)

and maidens that are his most typical and telling works – an ideal
vision of a way of life, dignified and serene of gait and gesture,
though whither the way is going is not clear. The frieze-picture
surely answered some deep need in the High Victorian imagination;
its chief inspiration was the Elgin marbles, the frieze from the
Parthenon in the British Museum (Leighton had a cast of this in
his house, and incorporated a glimpse of it in the self-portrait which
he sent to the shrine of great artists' self-portraits in the Uffizi at
Florence), but its active magic surely resided in its satisfying demon-
stration of an ideal pattern of ceremony and ritual, a stately queue
for eternity; the ceremony, in a materialistic society, rapidly becomes the object of the ritual. It is a format of painting by no means
confined to Leighton, but recurs in painters in modes as different as
Burne-Jones, while the examples that have survived best are those
by Albert Moore (no friend of the Academy, but of Whistler) in
those languorous ripples of drapery, flesh, and delicate colour that
blend into the monumental slumber of high noon [82].

   In subject-matter, Leighton's work is Mediterranean, and, after he
moved from fourteenth-century Italian themes, mostly of the
eastern Mediterranean. Here again, though no one else had his aloof
detachment, he was in company with other painters; the topo-

graphers and the scenic-view painters had already opened up this terrain, and so too had J. F. Lewis, anticipating the brilliance of colour of the Pre-Raphaelites in his pictures of the Middle East. For biblical accuracy, Hunt went to Palestine, and later Tissot followed him; Lear was busy in the Middle East. (The flavour of these sun-drenched subjects can still be experienced in context, in a few sur-viving houses, especially in the Midlands, where the collections built up through the mid-nineteenth century survive: gaunt great houses, sometimes now surrounded by the bleak expansion of industry, their dining-room stately with the giant portraits of the dynasty, the huge staircase-well glowing with the yellow visions of the Mediterranean in mammoth gilt frames.) But the most popular purveyor of classical figure painting was Alma Tadema, who, against a setting of scrupulously veined marble and blue sky, re-stated the anecdotal themes of earlier Victorian genre pictures, bringing a Victorian (and also rather Dutch) domesticity to ancient Rome.

A quick survey of English painting about 1880 would reveal a remarkably wide range of subject-matter; the escape-landscapes, in photographic detail, for tired urban eyes; the costume-pieces like real charades in paint; the scenic and archaeological paintings from the Mediterranean; the fay waif romance of Burne-Jones; the parade portraits; the anecdote of contemporary life, widening now to include documents more deeply socially-minded; flower-pictures, horse-pictures, the lot, all bowered in rather gross frames of un-relenting gilt. An art of material prosperity. Yet that is also of course a gross over-simplification. Leighton might be able at times to resolve matter and ideal in a processional, but the worried spirit of Watts is more typical of much that is best in High Victorian thought. It was Watts who wrote, in 1880, brooding on the present condition of Art:

The age is analytical and unsatisfied. Childlike enjoyment in anything for its own sake has almost departed, giving place in art at least to que-rulous questioning or frantic admiration. . . .

The archetypal image of the time was also provided by Watts in his most famous picture: *Hope* [83]. 'All the strings of her instru-ments are broken but one,' he wrote, 'and she is trying to get all possible music out of the poor tinkle.' It is the expression of the rather sumptuous agnosticism that shadows much of the work of

83. George Frederic Watts. *Hope* (second version), 1886 (57 by 45 in, 144·8 by 114·3 cm; Tate Gallery, London)

Watts's friend Tennyson; her draperies, acknowledging in their crinkle the Greeks, are doubtless as warm as a woolly and ulti- mately as vain; Watts probably did not know what the last frail string of her instruments signified, but then neither do we. It is of course over-literary, and yet, in spite of the alternations of praise and ridicule that have been showered on it, it remains a potent image for a great many people.

But this moral earnestness, however much paint was applied to it, never found its proper expression in paint in England. Against it, in the seventies, Whistler hurled thunderbolts in paint and even more in words (1877 was the date of Ruskin's invective against the 'coxcomb' who charged 200 guineas for 'flinging a pot of paint in the public's face', which provoked Whistler's famous libel action against him). And Whistler brings us in sight of, and all but in contact with, the stirrings of the new art in France – from Courbet to Impressionism, leading to Post-Impressionism and the revolution of Cézanne – that was to disrupt the Renaissance conception of painting. The truly prophetic dream in paint of the nineteenth century was not that of Leighton, or Watts, or the Pre-Raphaelites, but Courbet's vision of his own studio, now in the Louvre; this huge and extraordinary canvas shocked Redgrave cold in Paris in 1855 ('a house-painter . . . bad both in form and colour' – it was, essentially, coarse), but it places the painter plumb central at his easel, as master of the visible world. The world was to become to the painter more purely raw material, and his only loyalty to it lay in the duty of re-creating it in a shape valid as a picture.

Whistler, trained in France, was revolutionary enough in England, although his famous impressions of London dusks and fogs or of Venetian nocturnes [84] have no real relationship to the scientific theories of light on which the French Impressionists supported their enquiries. Yet his mood, and use of flat, almost silhouette, pattern, were new, and still more significant was his attitude to the subject-matter of his art. He refused to call the beautiful meditation on his mother a portrait: the subject of his picture, he said, might be of interest to him, but not to anyone else; the true subject was the form, the design, the colour – so he titled it, *Arrangement in Grey and Black* [85]. And although for most people now a considerable part of the charm of this picture resides in the contrast of the austere design with the typically Victorian sweetness of characterization of the old lady, it points forward to the ever-growing interest in purely pictorial values that has since turned picture-making so far away from 'nature' (as previously understood) in the last hundred years.

English art has come to terms with the European spirit of radical exploration only gradually and with reluctance (it was, for example, that erstwhile revolutionary, Holman Hunt, who wished to warn the world that 'the threat to modern art, meaning nothing less than its extinction, is Impressionism'), and a detailed and thorough investigation of its slow yielding to the new values has yet to be written, from 1885 onwards. That year saw the founding of the New English Art Club, to combat the old academic values, yet the Club's members maintained a curious indifference to the fundamental tenets of the artistic revolution in progress over the other side of the Channel, in spite of the fact that many of them worked at various times in France. Indifference is perhaps indeed the word, rather than incomprehension, for since the Elizabethans many British artists have refused, in their practice whatever they may have maintained in their theory, a final purity of visual logic in their work. Perhaps even now for most Englishmen, artists or amateurs, every picture had best tell a story; the emotional need is for illustration, for subject-matter with which they can identify, in which they can participate. Thus the landscapes of Wilson Steer recall the English countryside as rendered familiarly lovable to the nineteenth century by Constable and

84. James McNeill Whistler. *Nocturne in Blue and Silver: The Lagoon, Venice*, 1879–80 (20 by 26 in, 50·8 by 66 cm; Museum of Fine Arts, Boston, U.S.A.)

85. James McNeill Whistler. *Arrangement in Grey and Black*, 1871
(56 by 64 in, 142·2 by 162·6 cm; Louvre, Paris)

by Turner, more than they constitute a new vision of it. At its average level, such painting seems but a retarded and blurred expression of one of the low common denominators of so much post-Renaissance painting – of a comfortable and handsomely proportioned spirit in a comfortable and handsomely proportioned body, though wearing – in the case of the New English Art – superficial styles released from the fashion-houses of Paris. Even with the later counter-groups, the Fitzroy Street painters or the Vorticists, the visual logic is generally adulterated; thus in many of Wyndham Lewis's por-traits, for example, which are historically incomprehensible out of context with French Cubism, there is a most curious compilation of naturalism with chunky Cubist mannerisms. About 1907,

Augustus John, in small panels bold and brilliant with colour, was conducting what might seem to be an English Fauve revolution on his own, yet the colour always remains rooted in the subject-matter of the picture, representational, evocative of particular incident, in a way in which the colour of the Fauves, of Matisse or Dérain, no longer is. That detachment which seems to enable the great Continental masters to distil their vision to the essence, sometimes seems positively alien to British painters as they try with such heroic persistence to retain the flavour of the grape, even the bloom on its skin, in their brew. But such art as the best of John's is perhaps too easily overlooked by a generation for whom traditional humanist values have been shattered – by two world wars, by scientific, social, and psychological revolution. The conception of a natural order determined by the human scale, an order in which the human figure is the module, has gone; modern art, bending and breaking the appearance that confronts the artist's eye, is not content merely to shore its ruins with the fragments, but must weld them together in an impersonal creation that is impervious to human disaster: the logic of a Cubist painting, of a Mondrian, of a Pollock action painting even, is not subject to the shadow of the hydrogen bombs because we cannot identify with them as we can with even the most rigorously classic of paintings in the Renaissance tradition, a Poussin landscape for example. A Mondrian is a representation of a logic that, while it may be inhuman, is nevertheless an enduring order, a triumph over chaos. But the pessimism of this attitude was not congenial in Britain, and in the teeth of all evidence artists in Britain clung conservatively and tenaciously to belief in the old order. If their besetting sin is a genteel cosiness, the tougher spirits among them could strike splendid sparks off the objects that confronted them. The best portraits of the American-born Sargent, between 1885 and 1920, and those of John in the next generation, are witness to an incorrigible belief in the significance of the individual human being, the more individual, eccentric even, the better; that they are often also palpably unfinished is significant too. The visions of Stanley Spencer, sprung into angels out of dirt and gross flesh and green grass, never entirely transmute their origins, offending the rigorous eye with inconsistencies yet enchanting the reflexes of the average Englishman on the alert for the divinely human comedy. Only Sickert of all English painters between 1885 and 1939 (apart from Sargent, and a few living painters like Nicholson and Sutherland) holds any standing of reputation outside this country, his talent fined at its best by the example of his beloved Degas to that classic finality of precision, that enclosed monumentality that the French love. Whether he will outlast Spencer in the affection of the English remains for posterity to prove.

But that is to go far beyond the limits of this brief introduction, the true confines of which are two great revolutions – that of the Renaissance and that for which the name of Cézanne stands.

The course of English painting throughout, in relation to the main European stream, was capricious and often dangerously retarded in time, and too often much of it provincial in the bad sense, superficially imitative. Yet within it stand the achievements of Hogarth, of Reynolds, of Gainsborough, and of Lawrence; of Constable as of the great imported talents like Holbein and Van Dyck. And still the native Englishman may often find English painting most exciting, most mysteriously disturbing, when it is at its most boldly eccentric, most provincial, as with the late Elizabethans, with Blake, with Turner; when it thrusts away in exploration the outcomes of which are scarcely explicable in terms of European painting, and which Continental Europeans indeed find flawed, but which in the context of the still insular English culture, retain their own splendid validity.

For further reading

Many general studies of English painting exist, which cover the subject in greater detail than this short introduction can do. The best recent study is E. K. Waterhouse, *Painting in Britain 1530–1790* (Pelican History of Art, 1953; the companion volume on the later period is in preparation by Jonathan Mayne). Also indispensable are the volumes, now appearing, of the *Oxford History of English Art*, and those of the *Period Guides* (edited by R. Edwards and L. G. G. Ramsey; published by the *Connoisseur*, 1956 onwards).

Other works include:

BAKER, C. H. COLLINS, and CONSTABLE, W. G. *British Painting*, 1933

BINYON, L. *English Watercolours*, 1933

CROFT-MURRAY, E. *Decorative Painting in England*, two vols; 1962–4

EDWARDS, R. *Early Conversation Pieces*, 1954

GAUNT, W. *The Pre-Raphaelite Tragedy*, 1942

GAUNT, W. *Victorian Olympus*, 1952

IRONSIDE, R., and GERE, J. *Pre-Raphaelite Painters*, 1948

KLINGENDER, F. D. *Art and the Industrial Revolution*, 1947

OPPÉ, A. P. 'Art', in *Early Victorian England*, ed. G. M. Young, 1934

PIPER, D. *The English Face*, 1957

REDGRAVE, R. and S. *A Century of British Painters*, 1866 (ed. by Ruthven Todd, 1947)

REYNOLDS, G. *British Portrait Miniaturists*, 1952

REYNOLDS, G. *Painters of the Victorian Scene*, 1953

SITWELL, S. *Conversation Pieces*, 1936

STEEGMAN, J. *The Artist and the Country House*, 1949

TAYLOR, B. *Animal Painting in England*, 1955

WOODWARD, J. *A Picture History of British Painting*, 1962

Some works on individual artists are indicated in the Biographical Index.

Biographical Index

This index is confined to painters illustrated in the book

very slowly; elected A.R.A. 1819, R.A. 1829; exhibited successfully at Paris in the 1820s. The essential book is still C.R.Leslie's *Life* of him (ed. by J.Mayne, 1951, with bibliography).

COOPER, SAMUEL: 1609–72   23
Nephew and pupil of John Hoskins, the outstanding portrait-miniaturist in the tradition of Hilliard and Oliver; a tradition which Cooper enlarged in a revolutionary manner. Worked in London, the most fashionable miniaturist through the Interregnum and the Restoration, and had an international reputation. See in G.Reynolds, *British Portrait Miniaturists*, 1952.

COTMAN, JOHN SELL: 1782–1842   94
Painter of landscape in oils and watercolour. Born in Norwich, and always associated with Norfolk, though from 1834 he was Professor of Drawing at King's College, London. Exhibited at the R.A. only between 1800 and 1806. Leader with Crome of the 'Norwich School'. See S.D.Kitson, *Cotman*, 1937.

COZENS, ALEXANDER: 1717 (?)–86   90
Watercolourist in landscape. Born in Russia. Studied in Rome, and became a fashionable drawing-master in London; taught at Eton. Father of John Robert Cozens (1752–99), Beckford's chosen watercolourist and precursor of Girtin. See A.P.Oppé, *Alexander and John Robert Cozens*, 1952.

DEVIS, ARTHUR: 1711–87   67
Born at Preston, and specialized in the painting of small-scale portraits for a middle-class clientele. See S.H.Paviere, *The Devis Family of Painters*, 1950.

DOBSON, WILLIAM: 1610–46   20
Portrait-painter. Born in London, and studied probably under Cleyn. Worked in Oxford, painting the besieged Cavaliers, *c.*1642–6. See O.Miller and M.Whinney, *English Art 1625–1714* (Oxford History of Art, VIII), 1957.

ETTY, WILLIAM: 1787–1849   133
Painter of the female nude. Born at York; was a printer's apprentice at Hull before entering R.A. schools in 1807; worked under Lawrence; became A.R.A. 1824, and R.A. 1828. Lived a modest and retired life, devoted to his art. See D.Farr, *William Etty*, 1958.

162

EWORTH, HANS: working *c.* 1540–74

Portrait-painter. A Flemish painter from Antwerp, believed to be identical with one Hans Eworth (paintings associated with him are signed HE, but may be by two or more hands); working in England, mainly on portraits, from about 1544. See E. K. Waterhouse, in *Painting in Britain 1530–1790*, 1953.

FRITH, WILLIAM POWELL: 1819–1909   138

Born in Yorkshire, studied in London at Cass's school and at the R.A. schools; painted portraits and subject pictures, and later, topical genre scenes. Wrote a very successful *Autobiography*. Became A.R.A. in 1845; R.A. 1853.

GAINSBOROUGH, THOMAS: 1727–88   53, 80

Son of a crêpe-maker at Sudbury, worked under Gravelot in London before 1745, and was later influenced by Hayman; in the fifties painted mainly portraits at Ipswich, and moved in 1759 to Bath; exhibited at the R.A. but not after a quarrel in 1784. Moved in 1774 to London. For his living he depended always on portraits, but his chief love was for landscape. See W. T. Whitley, *Thomas Gainsborough*, 1915; Ellis Waterhouse, *Gainsborough*, 1958.

GIRTIN, THOMAS: 1775–1802   93

Watercolourist in landscape. Born at Southwark, and trained as topographical draughtsman under Dayes; toured British Isles and visited France; knew Turner and had some influence on his early work. See T. Girtin and D. Loshak, *The Art of Thomas Girtin*, 1954.

HILLIARD, NICHOLAS: 1547 (?)–1619   13

Portrait-miniaturist. Son of a Devonshire Goldsmith, and trained as a jeweller; visited France *c.* 1578, became court-miniaturist to Elizabeth, and engraved the Great Seal. Known to have painted also life-size, but no examples are known; his work declines after *c.* 1605. See J. Pope-Hennessy, *A Lecture on N. Hilliard*, 1949; E. Auerbach, *Nicholas Hilliard*, 1961.

HOGARTH, WILLIAM: 1697–1764   35

An insatiable Londoner, he trained as an engraver; between 1728 and 1732 began painting conversation and theatre pieces; his first comic series is of 1731. Painted life-size portraits with a fresh vigour. Visited Paris in 1743 and 1748 but was not impressed. Author of the *Analysis of Beauty*, 1753; appointed Serjeant Painter in 1757; his last years were clouded by quarrels with former friends, Wilkes and Churchill. He was closely allied to the literary talent of his time, particularly that of Henry Fielding. See R. B. Beckett, *Hogarth*, 1949 (the most reliable list; there is an enormous literature on Hogarth); F. Antal, *Hogarth and his Place in European Art*, 1962.

HOLBEIN, HANS (the younger): 1497–1543   8

German, born in Augsburg; went to Basle, 1514. The friend of Erasmus and Thomas More. In England 1526–8, and from 1531 until his death of the plague in London. Profoundly influenced by north Italian painting. In England he designed for engravers and metal-workers, and above all painted portraits. See P. Ganz, *The Paintings of Hans Holbein*, 1950.

HUDSON, THOMAS: 1701–79   31

Leading and typical portrait-painter of fashion between the eras of Kneller and Reynolds. A conservative but technically sound painter, proficient at the business of producing a likeness within a conventional formula. Reynolds started in his studio.

HUGHES, ARTHUR: 1830–1915   144

Born in London, and studied under Alfred Stevens and at the Royal Academy Schools; associated with the Pre-Raphaelites after 1850 but his career after *c.* 1865 is almost entirely obscure. See in R. Ironside and J. Gere, *Pre-Raphaelite Painters*, 1948.

HUNT, WILLIAM HOLMAN: 1827–1910   139

Born in London (Cheapside); worked as a boy clerk, then (1844) in R.A. schools, where he met notably the young Millais, with whom and Rossetti he founded the Pre-Raphaelite Brotherhood, 1848; he was the only member who worked on undeviating from his principles through a very long career. Made three visits to Palestine. His autobiography, *Pre-Raphaelitism and the Pre-Raphaelite Brotherhood*, 1905, is an essential source book.

KNELLER, SIR GODFREY: 1649 (?)–1723   29

German-born, studied in Holland and in Italy; came to England *c.* 1674, and became the most fashionable portrait-painter until his death. His output was enormous, aided by a large studio; knighted 1692, and made a baronet 1715. See in M. Whinney and O. Millar, *English Art 1625–1714* (Oxford History of Art, VIII), 1957.

LAWRENCE, SIR THOMAS: 1769–1830   98

Portrait-painter. Born in Bristol, became a boy prodigy, taking portraits in pastel from the age of twelve onwards. Came to London 1786 and was already an A.R.A. in 1791; succeeded Reynolds as Painter to the King in

1792, and elected R.A. 1794; knighted 1815, and President of the
Academy from 1820; visited Europe 1818–20 and painted the leaders of the
Allies. He was a tremendous worker, but his success was dogged always
by complete financial incompetence. See D. Goldring, *Regency Portrait
Painter*, 1951; K. Garlick, *Sir Thomas Lawrence*, 1954.

LELY, SIR PETER: 1618–80   25

Born in Holland and trained under de Grebber; came to England
c. 1643, and became painter to the Parliamentarians and then to the
Restoration Court; the most fashionable portraitist of his time; knighted
1680. See in M. Whinney and O. Millar, *English Art 1625–1714* (Oxford
History of English Art, VIII), 1957.

MILLAIS, SIR JOHN EVERETT: 1829–96   139

Born Southampton; entered R.A. Schools in 1840. Co-founder of Pre-
Raphaelite Brotherhood, and became A.R.A. in 1853; after 1860, his
style altered radically and he became a fashionable portrait-painter;
R.A. 1863, and President in 1896; created a baronet in 1885. See
J. G. Millais, *Life and Letters of Sir J. E. Millais*, 1899; R. Ironside and
J. Gere, *Pre-Raphaelite Painters*, 1948.

MOORE, ALBERT JOSEPH: 1841–93   150

Figure-painter. Born in York, of a family of professional painters. R.A.
schools in 1858; worked in seclusion in London, aloof from the Royal
Academy. A friend of Whistler. See A. L. Baldry, *Albert Moore*, 1894.

PALMER, SAMUEL: 1805–81   127

Painter of pastoral and landscape. Born in London; the decisive factor
was his meeting with Blake in 1824. Lived at Shoreham, Kent for about
seven years from about 1827, and there produced his most remarkable
paintings. In 1838 he married Linnell's daughter, and settled to a career
as a rather conventional watercolourist, and illustrator of Milton. See
G. Grigson, *Samuel Palmer*, 1947.

RAEBURN, SIR HENRY: 1756–1823   96

Born in Edinburgh, he became the principal Scottish portrait-painter,
largely self-taught; a brief Italian visit, 1785–7, did not affect him much.
A.R.A. 1812; R.A. 1815; he was knighted in 1822. See Sir W. Arm-
strong, *Raeburn*, 1901.

RAMSAY, ALLAN: 1713–84   71

Portrait-painter. Born in Edinburgh, much influenced by travels in Italy
in 1736–8; worked with Imperiali and Solimena. Settled in London in
1739, and became very successful. Painted little after 1769. See A. Smart,
The Life and Art of Allan Ramsay, 1952.

Portrait-painter. Born at Plymton Earl, Devonshire, apprenticed to Thomas Hudson in London when seventeen years old; practised on his own from 1743 till 1749, when he left for Italy and spent four years there making intensive studies. On his return he established himself as leading painter in a new style. First President of the Royal Academy, 1769, he delivered there his famous *Discourses*; knighted 1769. Painted little after 1789 owing to failing sight. See E. K. Waterhouse, *Reynolds*, 1941 (with bibliography); there is a good recent biography by Derek Hudson.

ROSSETTI, DANTE GABRIEL: 1828-82   139

Born in London, of Italian family. Studied at the R.A. and with Madox Brown; founder member of the Pre-Raphaelite Brotherhood. Later became somewhat of a recluse. A considerable literature exists on him as painter, poet, and personality. See especially H. C. Marillier, *D. G. Rossetti*, 1899; for the life, O. Doughty, *A Victorian Romantic*, 1941.

ROWLANDSON, THOMAS: 1756-1827   91

Born in London, trained at the R.A. and in Paris; caricaturist, and a very prolific producer of watercolour landscapes and figure studies, and illustrations, but dissipated his wealth and health. See A. P. Oppé, *Thomas Rowlandson; his Drawings and Watercolours*, 1923.

SCOTT, SAMUEL: 1702 (?)-72   47

Born in London (?), friend of Hogarth and Lambert; he began as marine painter, but after 1745 did mainly views of London. Retired to Ludlow, 1765. See in E. K. Waterhouse, *Painting in Britain 1530-1790*, 1953.

STUBBS, GEORGE: 1724-1806   59

Born in Liverpool; was in York c. 1744-52, where he began to study anatomy; paid a brief visit to Italy probably in 1754. From 1758 was engaged on the studies for his *Anatomy of the Horse* (1766); moved to London about 1759, and became A.R.A. in 1780, and R.A. 1781. He was always a horse-painter, though he made attempts at grand historical compositions with animals. See B. Taylor, *Animal Painting in England*, 1955.

THORNHILL, SIR JAMES: 1676-1734   28

Born in Dorset; established as a leading decorative painter soon after 1700. Worked notably at Greenwich and St Paul's; History-Painter to the King, 1718; knighted, 1720. He set up an artistic academy in his house.

TISSOT, (JAMES) JOSEPH JACQUES: 1836–1902   148
Subject-painter. Born in Nantes, studied at the Beaux-Arts in Paris,
knew Degas and Whistler. A strong sympathizer with the Commune in
1870, shortly afterwards fled to England. After a personal tragedy, he
left England about 1882 and later devoted himself to a famous series of
illustrations for the Bible. See James Laver, *Vulgar Society*, 1936.

TOWNE, FRANCIS: 1740–1816   88
Born in Exeter, and lived there most of his life, painting landscape both
in oils and watercolour, exhibiting in London. Toured Wales, Italy, and
Switzerland, and the Lakes. See A.P.Oppé, in *Walpole Society*, vol. VIII,
1920.

TURNER, JOSEPH MALLORD WILLIAM: 1775–1851   112
Landscape-painter. Born in London, son of a Covent Garden barber;
trained at the R.A. schools, and exhibited constantly from 1790 almost
till his death. Began as topographical watercolourist and oil-painter;
travelled extensively abroad particularly after the war in 1815. His early
landscapes influenced by Wilson, J.R.Cozens, and Claude. Elected
A.R.A. 1799, R.A. 1802. In 1826 he set up house in Queen Anne Street,
and lived a most secluded life, painting in prodigious quantity, caring
little whether his later, revolutionary work pleased the public. He be-
queathed his work to the nation. See A.J.Finberg, *Life of J.M.W.
Turner*, second edition, 1961 (with select bibliography); L.Herrman,
Turner, 1963

VANDYCK, SIR ANTHONY: 1599–1641   17
Born in Antwerp, closely associated with and profoundly influenced by
Rubens; he was briefly in England 1620-1, but thereafter in Italy and
Flanders until he settled here in 1632; he worked especially in portraiture
for Charles I and his court. For reproductions of his work see G.Gluck,
Van Dyck, 1931 (in German); also L.Cust, *Anthony van Dyck*, 1900, and,
especially for his English period, in M.Whinney and O.Millar, *English
Art 1625–1714* (Oxford History of English Art, VIII), 1957.

VAN DE VELDE, WILLIAM THE ELDER: 1611–93, and his son,   33
WILLIAM THE YOUNGER: 1633–1707
Marine-painters. The father was born at Leiden, Holland, and famous
for his grisaille studies of ships; he came to England with his son in 1673,
and both remained here until their deaths. They worked for Charles II,
James II, and William III. See in E.K.Waterhouse, *Painting in Britain
1530–1790*, 1953.

WATTS, GEORGE FREDERIC: 1817–1904   133

Portrait and subject-painter. Born in London, a child prodigy; he won first prize in the Houses of Parliament competition in 1843, and then visited Italy till 1847. Made an unsuccessful marriage with Ellen Terry, 1864. Elected A.R.A. and R.A. in 1867, and became the grand old man of British portraiture; O.M., 1902. See R. Chapman, *The Laurel and the Thorn*, 1945 (with bibliography).

WHISTLER, JAMES McNEILL: 1834–1903   153

Painter of landscapes and portraits; a very notable etcher. Born at Lowell, Massachusetts, starting as a draughtsman in the U.S. Coastal Survey; he never returned to America after leaving for Paris in 1855; knew Courbet, Degas, and Fantin-Latour. Settled in London, 1859. The *enfant terrible* of Victorian Painting. Pennell's *Life* is still the most important book.

WILKIE, SIR DAVID: 1785–1841   132, 135

Born at Cults, Fife; studied in Edinburgh and at the R.A. Schools; began by painting genre subjects and then many portraits. Became A.R.A. 1809; R.A. 1811; Painter in Ordinary to George IV, 1830. His style broadened after a visit to Italy and Spain, and was not so popular as his early manner. See in T.S.R. Boase, *English Art 1800–1870* (Oxford History of English Art, x), 1959.

WILSON, RICHARD: 1714–82   50

Born in Penegoes, Monmouthshire, the son of a clergyman; came to London, 1729, to study painting and set up practice as portraitist; when in Italy (*c.* 1750–7) he changed to landscape. A founder member of the Royal Academy, he never achieved widespread popularity. Retired to Wales at the close of his life. See W.G. Constable, *Richard Wilson*, 1953.

WRIGHT ('of Derby'), JOSEPH: 1734–97   57

Born at Derby, to which he returned after 1777. Trained as portraitist under Hudson in London, later painted many landscapes and specialized in forced light effects in subject-pieces; in Italy 1774–5. Made A.R.A. 1781, but quarrelled with the Academy soon after. See in E.K. Waterhouse, *Painting in Britain 1530–1790*, 1953.

ZOFFANY, JOHANN: 1734/5–1810   62

German, born in Frankfurt; he worked in Italy and Germany before settling in England about 1758, where he worked under Benjamin Wilson for a time; he was much favoured by George III, painting conversation pieces and portraits. Worked in India 1783–90. R.A. 1769. See in E.K. Waterhouse, *Painting in Britain 1530–1790*, 1953.

Sources of Illustrations

The publishers wish to make acknowledgement to the following, who have kindly given permission to reproduce works in their care:

The Trustees of the National Gallery, London (frontispiece, 1, 18, 33, 38–9, 42, 45, 64)

The Frick Collection, New York 21 (2)

Alys Luttrell, Dunster Castle, Somerset (3)

The National Portrait Gallery, London (4, 12, 73)

Victoria and Albert Museum, London, Crown Copyright (5, 46, 55, 57, 74)

The Collection of the Earl of Bradford, Weston Park, Shifnal, Salop (6–7)

The Trustees of the Tate Gallery, London (8, 16, 25, 27, 29, 30, 56, 58–61, 66, 67, 69, 72, 75, 78, 79, 81, 83)

Syndics of the Fitzwilliam Museum, Cambridge (9)

Hampton Court, London. Reproduced by Gracious Permission of Her Majesty the Queen (10)

Ministry of Works (11)

The National Maritime Museum, Greenwich, London (13–14, 19, 21)

Francis Tyrwhitt-Drake Esq. (15)

Sir John Soane's Museum, 13 Lincoln's Inn Fields, London (17)

The Governors of the Thomas Coram Foundation for Children, The Foundling Hospital, London (20)

Trustees of the Goodwood Collection, Goodwood House, near Chichester, Sussex (22–4)

Lord Mostyn (26)

The Earl of Inchcape (28)

The Earl Fitzwilliam (31)

The Viscountess Bury (32)

Lord Willoughby de Broke (34)

The Walker Art Gallery, Liverpool (35)

The National Gallery of Scotland, Edinburgh (37, 51)

The National Trust, Waddesdon Manor, Buckinghamshire (40)

The Royal Academy of Arts, Burlington House, London (41, 54)

The London County Council, Iveagh Bequest, Kenwood, London (43–4)

The Collection of D.L.T. Oppé and Miss Armide Oppé, London (47)

The British Museum, London (48, 50, 65, 70)

Sir Edmund Bacon, Bart, Raveningham, Norwich, Norfolk (49)

The Metropolitan Museum of Art, New York (52, 62)

Windsor Castle, Berkshire. Reproduced by Gracious Permission of Her Majesty the Queen (53)

Philadelphia Museum of Art (The John Howard McFadden Collection) (63)

The Museum of Fine Arts, Boston (68, 84)

The Ashmolean Museum, Oxford (71)

The City Museum and Art Gallery, Birmingham (76, 80)

Sir Colin Anderson (77)

William E. Kenrick Esq. (82)

The Louvre, Paris (85)

General Index